Learn from Me

Patterns and strategies in transformative healing prayer

Calvin R Tadema

Julie L Tadema

two worlds press

www.twoworldsmedia.com

Learn from Me: Patterns and strategies in transformative healing prayer.

© 2018 by Calvin Tadema and Julie Tadema

Published by Two Worlds Press, a division of Two Worlds Media of Portland, Oregon (www.twoworldsmedia.com).

Dedication

This book is dedicated to Rits and Pearl Tadema, our mentors and trusted advisers, and the source of our rich spiritual inheritance.

Acknowledgements

We want to thank our Church of the Heart for the spiritual support that has made this book possible. You have been a healing community through which we have learned about these patterns and the ways of God.

The Church of the Heart is made up of like-minded Christ-followers: Abide Ministries, Sonship Study, School of Prayer, and Kingdom Ministries. We also appreciate the support and encouragement from Vancouver Pillar Church, Montavilla Baptist Church, New Hope Community Church, and Grace Community Church.

We especially want to thank our Thursday evening Bible Study group for discussing these topics with us, and the Tuesday evening School of Prayer for putting these principles into practice. We have taught, discussed, explained and practiced these patterns and strategies with you, and enjoyed learning as we shared.

The board of directors for Master's Mind Ministry has been a great support: they are Ron and Ruth Hartford, Charlie and Karen Pudwill, Dan and Jody Mayhew, Dan and Linda Friesen, and Mark and Karen Hedinger. In addition, we acknowledge our Prayer Shield which is made up of prayer warriors from all over the globe. We feel the power of the Spirit unleashed by their worship and intercession.

Praise be to God!

Contents

Contents

Learn from Me

Introduction

Take My yoke upon you, and learn from Me. – Matthew 11:29a

The cover art for this book comes from one of my favorite oil paintings by my mother. She captured a scene from an event in her childhood that happened in the early 1940's.

My grandfather loved to plow the field near the road with his unlikely team. People would stop and stare, thoroughly amused by the odd sight of Slim, a huge white horse, and his yokemate Coin, the little donkey.

One day my mother, about eight years old, brought a coffee-time snack out to the field where my grandfather was working. She said, "Daddy, you should beat Coin to teach him a lesson. As soon as Slim starts to pull, Coin drops back and lets him do all the work. I know he's littler, but that lazy little donkey isn't doing his share!"

My grandfather was a gentle man. He smiled at my mom and said, "Don't you worry about Slim, dear. He loves to work and he's plenty strong enough to pull the plow. It's just that he likes to have Coin beside him. He doesn't need Coin to do any work, but Coin is his friend."

About five years ago my mother teamed up with my wife to teach at a women's retreat. She brought that painting as an illustration of being yoked with Jesus, as described in the Matthew 11 passage.

Learn from Me

The power of the Lord was with Him to heal. - Luke 5:17b

Imagine being yoked to Jesus while He ministered on earth, filled with the power to heal. What would you have learned as His wingman? The disciples, as eye witnesses, recorded many different healing strategies. Touching, affirming, anointing, commanding, casting out demons, and rebuking fevers were just a few of the ways He healed. Jesus knew what was in the heart of man and responded to each according to the need.

We can be yoked with Jesus in the spiritual realm and still learn from Him. His power alone heals, but we participate in the healing process much like Coin helped pull the plow. We are His friend and He invites us alongside as He works. Watch and listen through the Holy Spirit who reveals the heart of Jesus the Healer. Imagine yourself yoked to Him, able to see and feel His every move.

The purpose of the following examples and observations is to help you intercede effectively in prayer for others to receive healing. The essence of healing prayer is to ask the Spirit for direction and listen as He guides and brings truth. Prayer strategies follow these patterns. This book, however, is not intended to be a map for you to travel alone in prayer, but rather a compilation of observations and experience to help build your confidence in being yoked with Jesus.

For instance, I prayed with a man who wanted to be free from smoking. As we prayed for direction, the Lord brought to his mind a spirit of rebellion he had since his early teens. He was set free from his addiction when he was freed from that evil spirit. Since that time, we have noticed a pattern of rebellion associated with many addictions. Though we do not presume to find a spirit of rebellion in every case, we are not surprised when one is revealed by the Holy Spirit.

This book is also not intended to lead to opinions, assumptions or prejudices which lead to judgment. Judgment can be defined as one person holding another accountable with intent to condemn. We cannot pray for healing, which is an act of mercy, if we also desire punishment; that is the ineffective prayer of a double-minded man (James 1:7-8). Even a hint of judgment in our heart toward another disqualifies us from interceding on their behalf.

Our desire is that you learn from Jesus by taking His yoke upon you. Healing prayer is personal, powerful and thrilling. We share these patterns and offer prayer strategies to increase your confidence and enjoyment in intercession.

Rest for Your Souls

Come to Me, all who labor and are heavy laden, and I will give you rest, ... and you will find rest for your souls. – Matthew 11:28-29

Jesus gives a very comforting invitation to all who labor and are heavy laden. "Come, and I will give you rest. Come and you will find rest for your souls."

Sometimes when I think of rest, my thoughts go to vacation, sleeping in, and taking a break from work. But Jesus used a different word picture. He said to take His yoke upon you. A yoke is an instrument for work, a tool to harness and utilize power. His invitation is not to cease working but to work in an altogether new and different way.

Look again at the picture. You have probably already surmised that we are represented by the donkey in the picture. When Jesus invites us to "take His yoke upon us," we do so by slipping into the smaller yoke, just like Coin the little donkey. We are connected to Jesus and take our place beside Him. He slips into the bigger yoke like Slim, the powerful workhorse.

Now it is time to "work." Jesus provides the power and we walk alongside. Although we are not responsible for the work, He likes to have us there. When we are in that place there is rest.

We will quickly tire if we push ahead of Him. Even if we are confident of the direction, we are not equipped for the heavy lifting. We cannot do the work by ourselves. We must submit to His leading and match His pace.

We will quickly tire if we pull against Him in a different direction. Even if we are certain that we know an easier way, we cannot pull Him from the course He has established. We must submit to His leading and follow His direction.

My Yoke is Easy

For My yoke is easy, and My burden is light. - *Matthew 11:30*

Jesus proclaimed as fact that His yoke is easy and His burden light. He said it and it is true. What has been your experience in working with the Lord? Have you found His yoke to be easy and His burden light?

The idea of putting on a yoke sounds like hard work; in fact, when we are already tired, it seems counterintuitive. Many people in ministry get burdened and discouraged because they try to help others carry a heavy load. They are working for Jesus rather than with Him.

I can think of too many examples in my own life where I chafed at the yoke and strained at the burden. I took on too much responsibility and failed to follow His leading. I tried to guess the way He was going and meet or beat Him there, only to discover that I was missing information. Again, I needed to follow His leading.

Are you looking for rest? Stop dreaming about retirement, stop longing for a time to quit working. Instead, slip into His yoke and learn from Him. He will give you rest.

Think about Slim and Coin as you read this book and consider Jesus as the Healer who knows every prayer strategy.

Learn from Me

The "Learn from Me" indicator shown above is used throughout this book to identify examples. Stories of healing are praise-worthy and help us share specific prayer concepts. The names have been changed and we limit the scope of the example to focus on the most pertinent details to illustrate the lesson.

For example, we should be ready to pray with someone at any time and allow the Holy Spirit to guide our conversation.

I noticed Amy moving slowly and with difficulty as we gathered to pray for the opening of an annual women's conference. When I asked, she explained that she had been rear ended two weeks before and suffered whiplash from the accident. Immediately I sensed the Spirit encourage me to pray for her healing and to ask if she had forgiven the other driver. I obeyed.

"I never thought about forgiving her," she answered. "I've been upset that she was a distracted driver and her inattention caused me so much pain. I am willing to forgive her rather than hold on to any bitterness."

She offered a simple prayer of forgiveness, and I followed with a request that she be healed.

I prayed, "Lord, by Your stripes we are healed. I pray that Your stripes atone for the consequences of Amy's accident and that her neck be made right. I ask that You heal her muscles and bones and take away her pain."

"Thank you for praying, and reminding me to forgive," Amy said. "I feel more relaxed already."

A few months later I saw Amy at another function. She beamed as she walked briskly toward me. Bubbling with enthusiasm, she shared that her neck pain was completely gone the day we prayed. Then she added that her fear of driving had also been healed. After her accident she had felt tentative, especially at intersections, because of the pain in her neck. That fear and uneasiness was completely healed, too.

Notice in this illustration that the Holy Spirit initiated the prayer time. My willingness was immediately rewarded with a prayer strategy: to ask forgiveness for the other driver. We prayed as He directed and He made a complete healing.

This is an example of being yoked with Jesus, paying attention to His leading through the Spirit, and watching His power perform a miracle.

Intercession is the greatest ministry in the world! Jesus is the Healer and He invites us into meaningful participation with Him. Slip into the harness and learn from Him. You will be a witness to the supernatural.

PART I:

GENERAL

PRAYER STRATEGIES

Chapter One:
A New Creation

Therefore, if anyone is in Christ, he is a new creation. The old has passed away; behold, the new has come.
- 2 Corinthians 5:17

Did you see that!?

This spontaneous question is a call for a witness. It can be prompted by an amazing event or circumstance, such as a meteor streaking across the sky or a fleeting glimpse of a majestic animal. It can be a response to something startling, like a near-miss accident or logic-defying athletic performance. It can also be triggered by a dramatic change in a person as he or she is healed.

An intercessor is called to be witness to transformation. The Bible says: "Therefore, confess your sins to one another and pray for one another, that you may be healed (James 5:16)." Through the amazing circumstance of healing a person is changed into a new creation, as it says in 2 Corinthians 5:17. The new condition has come and we attest to the truth of the change.

One day I had opportunity to pray with a young man who suffered feelings of guilt. He had become a Christian three years before but deeply regretted the sinful choices he made growing up. The more he learned about his freedom in Christ the worse it seemed when Satan accused him of wrong. He still identified with the shame of his past.

I shared with him the good news that if anyone is in Christ he is a new creation, the old is gone and the new has come. I asked him to take an account of the ways he had offended God by his sinful choices and actions. Then I invited him to confess those offenses as sin against God and ask for forgiveness.

He prayed in simple terms and did a great job of presenting his sin before the Lord. The guilt from the Accuser turned into conviction of the Holy Spirit, and he apologized to God and asked Him for forgiveness.

I prayed after he finished, acting as a witness to a powerful spiritual transaction. Then I asked him how he felt.

"Bam!" He said.

We were outdoors, seated at a picnic table, and I was unsure of his answer. It could have been a young man's epithet to express emotion, so I leaned in and asked him again how he felt.

"Bam!" He repeated. Then he continued: "All the guilt and shame are gone! Bam! Just like that! I feel completely new, different, like a new man."

Therefore, if anyone is in Christ, he is a new creation.

The young man expressed it well when he said he felt completely different, like a new man. Creation is a supernatural act of God. Only God can make something new out of nothing, as He did when He created the heavens and the earth. A new creation is not a remodeled version of a former thing but something brand new.

The old has passed away; behold, the new has come.

The word "behold" is used to convey emphasis. It is a small Greek word in the original text that is sometimes translated as "Lo!" or "See!" or "Now!" It is an attention getter. It means that the action described is immediate and certain.

Behold, the new has come.

Perhaps "Bam!" is the new "behold."

In a spiritual sense this young man had been made new the moment he asked Jesus to come into his heart. The transaction is as good as done when a person is saved but the full benefit may not be realized immediately. He accepted forgiveness as we prayed together and Bam! the old passed away. He let go of his past and Bam! the new had come.

This is typical of the healed identity that comes with mind renewal. The Apostle Paul had this kind of transaction in mind when he wrote: "Do not be conformed to this world, but be transformed by the renewal of your mind, that by testing you may discern what is the will of God, what is good and acceptable and perfect (Romans 12:2)." Bam! You are a new person. Your old way of thinking and believing is replaced by the truth which is the perfect will of God.

I met up with that young man a few months later at a Men's Retreat. He greeted me enthusiastically and with a bright smile on his face he described the freedom of living in his new identity. The change looked good on him. This is an example of why we say it is a privilege to act as witness to this kind of transformation.

Fundamental Change

I blame our culture. We have been taught since grade school that change happens slowly over long periods of time. Scientific evidence is presented to prove the point, and it just makes sense. In a lifetime one can observe the erosion of sandstone, so it is common sense to project that same outcome over many lifetimes to something as hard as granite.

It is natural to assume personal development takes time as we grow and learn and apply our will to make improvements. On the other hand, a lack of attention tends to erode those improvements over time. Unfortunately, it seems to take less time to lose progress than gain it.

This kind of evolutionary thinking precludes the idea of a rapid fundamental change and argues against miraculous healing. But God is outside of time and is not constrained to a linear process. A day, year or thousand years are all the same to Him.

I'm certainly not against incremental improvement, and I believe strongly in the body's ability to restore itself to health given the chance. These are gifts God put into our design. We get smarter as we learn; we get stronger as we train; we get healthier as we fight off infection; and these things happen over time.

However, if anyone is in Christ, he is a new creation. This transaction is supernatural, which has no natural explanation.

The New Has Come

And God said, "Let there be light," and there was light. - Genesis 1:3

The language of the creation story is simple but conveys a powerful message. There was only formless void and darkness until God spoke, and then there was light. It describes a fundamental change in the environment. It is a dramatic scene that unfolds at the speed of light!

The original creation made something out of nothing. That's supernatural! A new creation is just as powerful and immediate, but (according to 2 Corinthians 5:17) something old passes away and something new takes its place. Specifically, the old identity dies and a new identity is raised in its place.

Bam! What was, is no more. The new that has taken its place was created from the beginning. "Behold!" and "Let there be light!" These are the words of supernatural creation, and immediately the new is revealed.

Transformation

Since, therefore, we have now been justified by His blood, much more shall we be saved by Him from the wrath of God. - Romans 5:9

We are forgiven when we are justified by His blood. That means the penalty of our sin has been paid. My dad used to say that when we are justified it is "just-as-if-I'd" never sinned. The old identity which includes the effects of the sin is changed by a spiritual transaction.

We know by faith that the transaction is complete in the spiritual realm. Everything that must be accomplished to atone for the sin has already been done and we are justified.

The sin no longer defines who we are. We are free to be the person God designed us to be.

The transformation is supernatural, and although the spiritual realm is unseen the change is immediate and permanent. We are a new creation. We have a new identity.

Our spirit conveys this newness to our soul. Like the spiritual realm, the emotional realm is not seen but is sensed through our mind, will and emotions. Our natural mind, subject to the fallen nature, may resist the supernatural truth. But it is certainly true, nonetheless.

Our natural bodies are subject to the physical realm, including time and consequences. Even so, the truth of our newness is made evident in our bodies.

This is the essence of healing. We are immediately changed, miraculously transformed, from the inside out.

Behold the New

For by grace you have been saved through faith. And this is not your own doing; it is the gift of God, not a result of works, so that no one may boast. - Ephesians 2:8-9

Transformation in the natural order depends on your own doing. It is a "result of works" through which you use your mind, will and emotions to affect change in your identity. We expect this change to take time and that regression is as likely as progress.

"Self-help" programs and religious behavior are based on the premise that we can affect change and, like evolution, we hope the change will be for the better. The causes and effects of these changes can be explained with natural laws and theories, but no supernatural power is used in this approach.

Stop trying to evolve; and stop expecting or demanding that someone else evolve. Rather, accept the gift of God: the supernatural gift of re-creation.

I prayed with a man who had been a slave to sin for many decades. His life was a mess and the consequences of his fallen nature were obvious. Once he understood the gift that God offered there was no hesitation. He confessed his sin and asked for forgiveness while I listened as a witness. He received a renewed mind and was set free from his addictions. He could not stop smiling. Behold (Bam!), the new had come.

A few weeks later I met with him and his wife to address her concerns about his past. She acknowledged that the change in his mind, will and emotions was dramatic, but she worried that he would slip back into his old ways. She wondered what needed to be done to protect against this possible recidivism.

"Has he ever tried to change his behavior and live a different life before?" I asked.

"Oh, yes. Many times," she said. "That's why I'm worried about him slipping back. I believe he wants to change, but I don't think he's able."

"Honestly, I don't think he's able either. If it were up to him, I wouldn't hold out much hope," I said softly. Then I added: "You said you've seen some dramatic change in him the last few weeks. Do you think he finally figured out how to pull it off?"

"No, not really. I can't explain what's happened, but it's not him."

"I agree. It had to be supernatural, because it's way more than he could do. That's the good news for you. Don't be worried, he wasn't healed of his own doing. It was a gift from God! You don't have to have faith in your husband, but there's every reason to keep your faith in God."

Bam! He is a new man. You cannot explain it, but you can believe it.

Identity in Christ

We have been engaged in healing prayer ministry for more than a decade, and the number one issue boils down to an identity crisis. People do not know who they are designed to be so they create an identity and personality. Children play make-believe, sometimes quite elaborately. Pre-teens may experiment with a variety of personas in search of something special, and often are pigeonholed by others. Young adults may continue to cast about for an identity, putting on airs to project an image.

Even adults are confused about their identity. They pretend that their title or role defines them: "I'm a doctor, or a pastor, or a teacher, or a homemaker, etc." But it leaves them looking for more. They lose themselves in hobbies or entertainment: "I'm a Seahawks fan, or a golfer, or a fly-fisherman, or a talk-show host, or a reality TV wannabe." They are hoping something will make them special, but in all these cases they come up empty.

At a loss for an authentic identity, many turn to the opinions of others for guidance. They are playing to an audience trying to find acceptance. The pattern begins early, especially for those who have a desire to please. Soon they make guesses about who they should be based on the slightest hints from friends or even less reliable sources. Any semblance of their true identity emerging from that morass is purely coincidental.

Since people can be influenced by the opinion of strangers, imagine the power of a message that comes from an authority figure such as a parent, teacher, or boss. In fact, some adults are still trying to meet their parents' expectations, even though the parent's authority over them has long since expired.

Others are so desperate for an identity they cling to the closest thing they can find to a definition of self. They grab onto anything that provides reason for their existence. They are susceptible to accepting a label as an identity, especially if it comes from an authority.

For example, a doctor uses a name to describe a collection of symptoms. We refer to this as a diagnosis. It is useful for discussing a person's condition and comparing it to data collected about others with similar symptoms.

However, when people are desperate for an identity they may stretch a diagnosis into a definition of who they are. They might think: "I'm 'clinically depressed.' This finally explains my feelings, my behavior, and my future. The search for my identity can be over. Now I know who I am."

Wrong!

We are who God says we are. When we act in a different identity there is conflict which is expressed as pain in the physical, emotional and spiritual realms. We must be reconciled to God through Christ Jesus to become the person God designed us to be. Then the conflict ceases and we are filled with peace.

— *Learn from Me* —

Rose came for prayer because of her anger issues. She was in her mid-twenties but acted rather immature with very low self-esteem and no self-confidence. She had trouble building healthy relationships and tended to appease others for a while, and then would lash out at them in frustration. She hoped for a better life.

We asked God to reveal the root issue of her anger and relational problems, and she quickly described a source of frustration from when she was growing up. Her mother was impossible to please, but the thing that hurt the most was when she was told to go to her room anytime she began to express herself.

I asked her to recall the frustration and allow God to show her if there were other thoughts or memories related to the feeling.

"I felt like a big fat failure," she said. "Mom always made snide comments about people, especially overweight people, calling them losers and slobs. I took it personally, because I was kinda frumpy, a loner, and a disappointment to her."

Rose went on to explain that her dad never took her side. He was there, but would not oppose her mom, even when he saw how much the comments and judgment hurt. She felt unloved and stuck in an environment that was emotionally and personally stifling.

I invited her to forgive her mom and dad for poor parenting, lack of nurture, judgment and criticism. Rose considered that offer seriously before agreeing, but when she had released the offenses of her parents it made a difference in her heart. She smiled broadly and expressed how much freer she felt.

"Rose, you came to believe that you were a big fat failure. That's a tough identity to live with. Would you be willing to ask God for the truth?" I asked.

She nodded and we went right to prayer. She described the picture God put in her mind. It was of a young, carefree girl playing with some friends. She remembered being that girl and how it felt to be free. She smiled and confessed that this was a picture of her true identity.

Rose began to live in that new identity. She got her driver's license, a new job, and built meaningful friendships with peers at church. Even though her mom had stifled her creativity and modeled harshness, Rose discovered that she is expressive, artistic, nurturing and compassionate. The new identity is a much better fit because it is God's design for her.

Mind Renewal

... You have put off the old self with its practices and have put on the new self, which is being renewed in knowledge after the image of its Creator. - Colossians 3:9-10

Healing, at its core, means to be reconciled to God in Christ Jesus. The old self, which is the false identity, has to be replaced with the new self, which is the true identity. Earlier in the third chapter of Colossians, Paul proclaims that we have died to the old nature in order to be resurrected with Christ in new life. This is the supernatural exchange through which we are created anew by God.

You are what you think. Your current identity is formed and controlled by what you believe to be true. This is your paradigm, your belief system, in which you put your faith. That is why it is so important to consider the source of your information about yourself. Do not put your faith in the reckless opinions of others, misguided intentions from family, misinterpreted signals from peers, or the misapplication of a diagnosis. Put your faith in God by being renewed in knowledge according to the image of your Creator.

Simple Mind Renewal Outline

1) *Ask the Lord to identify the current pain or conflict.*
2) *Focus on the conflict and ask how this makes you feel, or what it tempts you to do.*
3) *Interrogate, or question, the emotion or action to discover the underlying belief.*
4) *Interrogate, or question, the belief by asking how you came to believe it to be true.*
5) *Surrender the belief to Christ and ask for His truth.*
6) *Accept the Truth in place of the old belief.*
7) *Check to see that the original pain or conflict has been resolved to peace.*

Pursuing mind renewal requires thinking a different way; to exchange one paradigm for another. It is vitally important then to know what needs to be replaced and what needs to be confirmed. We call it brainwashing when one person causes another to accept his worldview. We call it education when the intent is to adapt one's worldview to truth.

Pilate asked the right question of Jesus: "What is truth?" Healing prayer asks the same question about what one believes to be true.

How do you know what you believe? You see the evidence expressed in how you feel and how you act.

We use the term "interrogate" quite intentionally because of the strong message it conveys. Interrogation is a determined and intentional method of questioning. Who are you? Why are you here? What is your purpose? Whose authority are you under? We use powerful questions and demand answers to get to the root underlying an issue.

Interrogate Your Emotions and Actions

Emotions are neither good nor bad; they are simply a response to what you believe to be true. If you believe your life is in danger you will experience fear. If you believe you have lost something of value you will feel sadness. If you believe you are about to receive something of value you will feel excitement. Your emotions respond to your expectations.

We sometimes say "historical accuracy is overrated" because your emotions do not prove something to be true, they respond to what you believe in the moment. For example, if a friend approaches you on your birthday with a gift bag you will feel anticipation because you believe you are about to receive a gift. If you discover that the gift is for someone else, your emotions will change as quickly as your belief. Your former excitement was not wrong, just short-lived. The point is, your emotion is an accurate indicator of your belief.

The same is true with your actions. You respond to what you believe to be true. If you believe your life is in danger you will either fight or run, depending on your personality and the situation. If you discover that your life is not in danger, despite your fear, your actions will change accordingly. Your initial reaction was not wrong, it was appropriate for what you believed to be true in the moment. However, when the new truth replaced the initial assumption your reaction changed.

Whether we interrogate emotions or actions, the goal is the same: What do you believe to be true that causes you to act or feel this way?

Interrogate Your Beliefs

What do these words have in common: believe, know, faith, hope, conviction, opinion, trust, and confidence? Most people consider them to be near synonyms or similar terms that describe the ingredients of a paradigm. Yet there can be confusion in the nuances of meaning.

For purposes of mind renewal, we are interested in a person's guiding beliefs. These are convictions or opinions that are held in the heart and have a conscious and subconscious effect on emotions and behaviors. They should not be confused with views or ideas of which we are aware in our mind, for these latter concepts inform but do not actually guide us.

For example, an adult may recite the truth that God will never leave them nor forsake them. If you ask if they believe that to be true they may quickly affirm it because they are aware that the statement is from the Bible. However, if you ask if it feels true to them you may get a different answer. This has been called the "head-heart split." In our head are all the "right" answers that we have stored for later recall. In our heart are guiding beliefs, and these are the ones we must interrogate or challenge.

— Learn from Me —

Martin struggled with panic attacks, and a recent episode prompted him to schedule a prayer appointment. I opened with prayer and God confirmed that we should consider this conflict, so we began to interrogate his emotion of panic.

He described an incident that began with a caution, grew into worry, then became anxiety, and finally a paralyzing panic. He believed that the panic attack could take over his body and he would not be able to protect himself. I asked God to reveal how he came to believe this to be true.

In response he recalled the first time he experienced a panic attack. He was in his late teens, visiting with some friends for a few days while trying to figure out how to leave home for good. It had been a rocky time with his dad that led up to this. He was alone in an unfamiliar house, and he began to consider the enormity of his decision. The thought of independence, while exciting on the one hand, was daunting on the other. His thought grew to worry, his worry to anxiety, and then he had a full-blown panic attack. He could not move and felt as if he were detached from his body.

We prayed for clarity and I asked the Spirit to reveal the object of his fear. Surprisingly he realized it was a fear of "fear." He believed a panic attack could take over his body, and its onset was outside of his control. He had been trying to guard against that possibility by eliminating thoughts that might lead to any form of fear. Of course, this was an impossible assignment.

I prayed: "Lord, Martin believes that he could be paralyzed by a panic attack, and that this could happen at any time, and that he has no control over it. Would you now reveal Your truth to him in this matter?"

Martin kept his head bowed for a few moments but when he looked up his face had changed. I asked him to describe what the Lord had revealed to him.

"While you were still praying, I remembered how it felt when I was planning to leave home. I had never been on my own before and didn't know if I could handle it. I was afraid my dad would cut me off completely," he said. "But then it dawned on me: I was an immature eighteen-year-old then, and my decision seemed huge to me. I'm not that scared little kid anymore. God has been faithful to protect and guide me."

"That sounds like real truth to me," I responded. "How does that make you feel?"

"Oh, I feel great." Then he added, "I know a verse that says 'Cast all your cares on Me.' I know I can deal with the little fears, and anything that grows into anxiety I'll call a 'care' and cast it on Him!"

I reminded Martin that fear is just an emotion, and it is a response to what you believe to be true. This is normal and healthy. However, a "fear of fear" is a scheme of the enemy. The devil cleverly inserts a fear of an emotion, rather than a belief. This then quickly becomes a vicious cycle. Once you enter the vortex of fear it spirals out of control, being fed by the very fear it creates.

I led him in a prayer to command the spirit of fear to leave in the name and authority of Jesus. Then we talked about how to defend against any future attack. Martin has been free from panic attacks since that time.

Be Reconciled to God

Reconciliation is a banking term. It means that an owner's record of debits and credits matches the bank's record. They are in agreement.

Mind renewal is a way to describe the reconciliation process in spiritual terms. We are reconciled to God when our version of the truth matches His. When a discrepancy exists, we can assume the fault is ours, not God's. Therefore, we take our thoughts captive to make them obedient to Christ (2 Corinthians 10:5).

The thoughts, beliefs, and truths we carry have accumulated throughout our life. Some are convictions gained by careful consideration of God and His ways. Others are firm opinions gathered from spurious sources. Still others are conclusions we have jumped to, perhaps with very little to go on.

We can easily change a conclusion when reliable information is introduced. We call that education. It takes a little more effort to change an opinion that has been influenced by an authority figure, like a parent or teacher. Our convictions, however, are the most difficult to change. They are hard-won beliefs that resist change. In fact, the more they cost us emotionally or physically, the harder they are to change.

We must replace a belief at the point in time in which it was inserted. In the example above, Martin was eighteen when he came to believe that he could not handle the responsibility of being an adult. Over the next ten years he proved he could because he lived on his own. In his head he knew his fear was not true, but his heart still held the belief that had been adopted when he was eighteen.

When the Lord revealed truth to him, it was retroactive back to the time the false belief first entered his mind. Though his twenty-eight-year-old mind could reason from experience that he was able to handle the responsibility of adulthood, these views and ideas did not override his previous conclusion. It was necessary for God to renew his heart-held belief by releasing fear from his eighteen-year-old mind.

We see this pattern no matter how early in one's life the guiding belief was inserted. One of my favorite prayer moments was with a woman in her late eighties who experienced mind renewal of her four-year-old mind. She believed she was easily confused and could not give the right answer when tested. This conclusion was drawn because she felt like she did not know how to answer when she was four.

God showed her that it was an historic event and that although her conclusion was true then, it was not a lifelong condition. She had changed but her heart-held belief had not. She agreed with God's assessment, released that guiding belief, and accepted as true that God had given her a mind which is entirely capable of clear thought and reason. God is outside of time, and He is able to place the truth exactly in the historical context it is needed.

This is a very important point for dealing with a head-heart split. The adult mind has the experience and capacity to draw a different conclusion than the child mind. Yet, when the conflict is resolved or rationalized by the adult mind it does not transfer back in time to change the conclusions of the child mind. When we try to rely on our logic and reason to override the process we are cheated out of replacing the false belief with the truth.

It is fascinating to watch the Holy Spirit provide insight to a person through the ages of their development. God is outside of time. I have seen Him speak truth to the adult mind and then the child mind, back and forth, without any sense of discontinuity. Through the process, the person's whole mind is renewed and their thoughts are reconciled. The person becomes a new creation.

Chapter Two:
The Role of Faith

And Jesus said to him, "'If you can'! All things are possible for one who believes." Immediately the father of the child cried out and said, "I believe; help my unbelief!" - Mark 9:23-24

The gospel of Mark tells the story of the desperate father who wanted Jesus to heal his son. He asked Jesus if He had enough compassion to do something, and Jesus replied by asking if he had enough faith to receive it. In other words, the limiting factor was not Jesus' compassion but the father's ability to believe.

Mark's gospel is written in a crisp style with an economy of words. When I imagine myself as that father I think I would have cried out and said: "I want to believe, I choose to believe, I have to believe. I do believe with everything I've got, and if that's not enough, I believe You can give me more!"

Jesus commanded the deaf and mute spirit to come out of the boy and he was healed. There were some theatrics involved, and a crowd of people was gathering, but the bottom line is that the boy was set free. Mark told the story to prove that Jesus had compassion and that the father had enough faith to receive what he asked.

Faith that Heals

And Jesus said to him, "Recover your sight; your faith has made you well." - Luke 18:42

Many times, Jesus made a connection between a person's faith and healing. The blind man begging on the side of the road called out in faith, and his faith made him well. The Samaritan leper was healed by his faith (Luke 17:19), and the woman who touched His garment (Matthew 9:22), and the sinful woman who anointed His feet (Luke 7:50) are also examples of healing specifically tied to faith.

Jesus quickly gained a reputation for having compassion and healing all who came to Him. The reports went abroad and great crowds gathered to hear Him and to be healed of their infirmities (Luke 5:15). The more He healed, the easier it was for the masses to believe.

A type of faith-momentum happened. As some people were healed by faith others came to believe they could be healed, too. His fame spread throughout all Syria, and they brought Him all the sick, those afflicted with various diseases and pains, those oppressed by demons, epileptics, and paralytics, and He healed them (Matthew 4:24).

Lest you think it was all about Jesus and His compassion, we read the account of His return to His hometown. What a huge contrast! What a letdown!

> *And He did not do many mighty works there, because of their unbelief. - Matthew 13:58*

The people who needed healing were unable to receive it because of their unbelief. They certainly had heard about His miracles and were amazed by His teaching, but they could not see beyond His past. To them He was just the "son" of Joseph the carpenter. Rather than cry out for Him to help their unbelief, they treated Him with skepticism and contempt.

Faith has an important role to play in healing prayer today, just as it did in the time of Jesus. Skeptical and suspicious people may be in desperate need of healing but unable to receive it.

At the beginning of this chapter I referenced the father with a little bit of faith and a desire for more. The story begins before this, however. While Jesus and a few of His disciples were on the Mount of Transfiguration, the rest of the disciples were down in the valley among the people. Though they had tried, they failed to help the father. For some reason, the healing could not take place. I believe the reason was unbelief.

And when they came to the disciples, they saw a great crowd around them, and scribes arguing with them. - Mark 9:14

The disciples were there as representatives of Jesus, but the scribes argued with them. It was a contentious setting, a battle between two doctrines regarding the way to receive God's healing. The father was torn between the factions and, like a double-minded man, was unstable in his ways. His need to believe was undermined by the religious authorities.

Sometimes we are faced with similar circumstances. We want to pray for healing with someone who needs the touch of our Lord, but the environment is filled with conflict. The world does not believe in Jesus, and even some who profess to know Him do not understand His compassion. They argue or waffle between opinions and are unable to receive the great gift. Like those in Nazareth, they will not see many mighty works because of their unbelief.

When the crowd wondered why the disciples could not cast out the deaf and dumb spirit from the boy, Jesus explained.

And He answered them, "O faithless generation, how long am I to be with you? How long am I to bear with you? Bring him to Me." - Mark 9:19

He did not accuse the father of unbelief, though there was self-admitted weakness there. He did not accuse the disciples of unbelief, though they too recognized their weakness. He called out the whole faithless generation, meaning the crowd that had gathered. Like His hometown, the environment was conducive to doubting rather than believing.

Then He said, "Bring him to Me." Jesus knew He had the power to heal. He ignored the crowd and narrowed His focus to the father. At that moment it was just between the two of them, and they volleyed the statement: "If you can." In other words, the father was asking Jesus if He could, and in the affirmative Jesus asked him if he could. The two believed, the son was healed, and the crowd was excluded from the transaction except as witnesses.

Learn from Me

Sometimes we, as intercessors, need to employ the same strategy. The noise and commotion of this faithless generation would distract or dissuade the one who is trying to believe. Some of the arguments are religious in nature, which is no different than two thousand years ago. Some of the arguments are scientific, which stem from the false god of reason. I believe Jesus answered the father's request to help his unbelief by isolating him from the opposition and distraction.

> *Moses spoke thus to the people of Israel, but they did not listen to Moses, because of their broken spirit and harsh slavery.* - *Exodus 6:9*

Often an unbelief challenge happens before the prayer appointment. The person who is stuck in his sin and cruel bondage may have lost hope that anything good could happen to him. It is a lie from the evil one that keeps him from seeking the truth. As long as he believes nothing can change, he will stay in his captivity.

When God promised to release Israel from slavery in Egypt, He sent Moses to tell them the good news. But they did not listen to him because of their discouragement and cruel bondage (Exodus 6:9). People who have been trapped in addictive behavior or suffer from enslavement to fear may have a broken spirit just like the descendants of Abraham. The good news of their imminent release comes and they are unable to listen to it. They may be tempted to skip the appointment or cancel it at the last minute.

Four hundred years of slavery and twenty generations of bondage wiped out all thought or memory of independence, freedom and dignity for the people of Israel. Moses brought them good news of hope and healing, but they did not listen to him. They could not hear the message because of their discouragement and cruel bondage.

This verse really came alive to me several years ago. My sister, Laura, was the director of Acres of Diamonds, a Christian ministry for homeless women. We had been talking about the importance of accessing God's healing power to transform these precious lives. For some reason there was resistance. The women did not have the faith that they could be healed nor the hope that anything could change.

I realized then that, like the people of Israel, they could not listen to the good news because of their broken spirit and harsh slavery. They were trapped in a culture of addictions and hopelessness. They were enslaved to their sinful ways and stripped of dignity by their homelessness. They were without hope.

God gave the people of Israel hope by doing mighty works among them. The plagues were followed by His miracles as they were led out of slavery to become a kingdom of priests.

This book is filled with testimonies of God's miraculous power. We have been witnesses to many mighty works and love to share the good news that He heals the broken hearted and raises up the downcast. We share these stories to bring hope.

When a person struggles with pain or trauma, whether in the spiritual, emotional or physical realms, it is the most pressing thing in their life. If they have been enslaved to pain or suffering for any length of time they may become discouraged or have a broken spirit. Then they may lose hope and become unable to hear the good news that God heals.

The role of the witness is to offer hope. You are saying to them: "You may believe your situation is hopeless, but I am willing to pray with you because I know God has a hope and a future in mind for you." This is a way of inviting the person who needs prayer to come and borrow your hope if they don't have enough of their own.

Protect your sense of hope at all times. Keep your mind free from offense, judgment and condemnation about the person because those thoughts kill hope immediately. Feed your mind with the Truth of the gospel because it contains hope. Remind yourself of the things God has done in the past and give Him praise. Exercise unconditional love because love hopes all things (1 Corinthians 13:7).

Faith Challenges

After these things God tested Abraham and said to him, "Abraham!" And he said, "Here I am." He said, "Take your son, your only son Isaac, whom you love, and go to the land of Moriah, and offer him there as a burnt offering on one of the mountains of which I shall tell you." - Genesis 22:1-2

God really loved Abraham. I do not see this request as some kind of pass / fail test to determine Abraham's worthiness or loyalty. God knew that Abraham really loved Him, too. I believe this trial was a sure-fire way to prove it to Abraham, not God.

A similar scenario is revealed to us through the book of Job. God knew how much Job loved Him and proclaimed it to the devil. The challenge served to prove the truth to Job and the devil, not God.

Our relationship with God will improve as soon as we begin to understand His deep love for us, and that He is willing to send us a faith challenge for our benefit, not for His. We say we have faith, but how do we know? Faith survives under challenge.

We have a saying: "Your healing is only theoretical until it is put to the test." We encourage people with these words, so when the test comes it serves to prove the truth rather than shake their faith. That is the benefit of a faith challenge. When you have risen to the challenge it proves to you and anyone else watching that your faith is real.

Belief

One way to accept a faith challenge is to put your new belief into practice. We are reconciled to God through Christ by the renewing of our mind. God takes a conclusion from our paradigm and replaces it with His truth and then we are made right with Him in our way of thinking. However, we need to apply the new truth of our changed paradigm before we will receive any benefit from it.

We say "I'll believe it when I see it" but it is more accurate to say "I'll see it when I believe it" because we see what we believe.

Our mind constantly filters our observations to align with our pre-existing conclusions. Unless we activate our renewed mind, our future observations will be subject to the same old prejudices.

— Learn from Me —

Elizabeth wanted to get her GED, hoping that it would open doors for a better paying and more fulfilling job. She was fifty years old and had been stuck in minimum wage and menial labor positions. It seemed hopeless to her because of her limitations and feelings of inferiority. She was discouraged to the point of depression.

I prayed with her about these feelings and we asked God to reveal what she believed that caused her such distress. She recalled the dysfunction and trauma in her family of origin that left her with a spirit of confusion. Her parents raised her but emotionally abandoned her. School was very hard for her and there was never any help. She failed classes, felt stupid, and was looked down upon by classmates and teachers alike. She began to act out in her self-loathing.

She said: "I always felt like I was unable to learn, that my mind didn't work properly. Because of that, I believed I didn't deserve any help or support. I was on my own, and there was so much I couldn't do because I was mentally deficient."

We took those thoughts captive and asked God to reveal truth in their place.

"I know I was always slow in school, but God just said I am wise and I have good gifts," she said. "I also think that since God answered me that means I can get help. I don't have to do it on my own. God can help me, and He can have others help me with how to get started, the paperwork, and even how to study."

"Elizabeth, you've wanted to get your GED for many years but couldn't because you thought you were unable and unworthy. How will you know things have changed?" I asked.

Learn from Me

"Well, God also told me to quit gossiping because it is a form of judgment. When I gossip about others I am keeping them stuck in their old ways, but I'm keeping me stuck in my old ways at the same time. I don't want to be stuck anymore," she answered quickly.

A few weeks later, Elizabeth told me she was getting started on her GED and had started running again to get back into shape. She looked forward to hiking again next summer.

Once she embraced the truth that she is wise and had good gifts, she was able to live in her true identity. The spirit of confusion was taken away as she discarded those old beliefs and started living as a new person.

Confession

When anyone hears the word of the kingdom and does not understand it, the evil one comes and snatches away what has been sown in his heart. This is what was sown along the path. · Matthew 13:19

God reveals His truth to us by putting His word directly into our heart so it bypasses our preconceived ideas and conclusions. However, the evil one tries to snatch it away before we can understand it. Jesus implied by the parable that understanding the word was equivalent to the seed taking root. Then that word of truth becomes part of our paradigm because it brings understanding.

Because, if you confess with your mouth that Jesus is Lord and believe in your heart that God raised Him from the dead, you will be saved. · Romans 10:9

One of the quickest ways to activate our faith and accept the truth in our heart is to make a confession. A clear connection exists between believing and confessing, as the Apostle Paul described in the letter to the Romans. We know what we believe when we hear ourselves speak it aloud. Our thoughts become more tangible and permanent as we verbalize them into the physical realm.

The intercessor can facilitate this process by asking recipients to express the truth God has given them. At times they may struggle for words but the patient prayer warrior will wait for the confirmation. Encourage them to speak it and then help them to articulate it further. The seed that takes root is not so easily snatched away by the evil one.

— *Learn from Me* —

Dustin was addicted to drugs. He became dependent on prescription drugs after surgery and had not learned how to return to a drug-free life. We asked God to reveal the source of the pain, and immediately the unresolved conflict with his dad came to mind.

"I was never good enough for my dad," he said. "No matter how hard I tried, he would find fault with me. At some point, I think I gave up trying to please him. It was impossible."

We took that realization to prayer and asked God to show Dustin what he believed to be true in the midst of that conflict.

"I believed there was something wrong with me and that there was no way I could be anything but a failure."

"Lord, Dustin has confessed the belief that he can only be a failure. Would You please show him the truth that he needs to know?" I prayed.

"I saw an image of Jesus while you were praying," he said. "He looked right at me and smiled."

I waited for him to say more, but he stopped there. I asked, "What does that mean to you? Why would Jesus smile at you?"

"It was a friendly smile. He thinks I'm OK; that there's not something wrong with me."

"Does that feel true? Would you say that a smile from Jesus is proof that you are not a failure?"

"Yes," he affirmed. "It feels true that Jesus doesn't see me as a failure. It feels true that according to Him I'm OK."

Learn from Me

That was the turning point for Dustin's healing. He activated his faith by speaking aloud the mental image God gave him in answer to his prayer. The truth took root as he applied the meaning to his life. He was set free from his addiction that day and began to live a new life with a renewed mind.

Obedience

A step of obedience is the classic faith challenge, as described above in the account of Abraham and Isaac. This was a true test of character for Abraham and it proved his faith. The Bible is filled with other examples where an act of obedience is the key to the release of supernatural power for healing.

For instance, Elisha gave Naaman the instruction of dipping seven times in the Jordan River to be cleansed from leprosy. The miraculous healing happened as soon as he obeyed. In this example a condition had to be met to demonstrate faith.

The woman with an issuance of blood believed she would be healed if she could just touch the hem of Jesus' robe. As soon as she was able to act on that faith her healing was realized. The action proved the faith that was otherwise invisible. In each of these examples, the act of obedience proved the existence of the faith and released its power.

— Learn from Me —

Cathy came for prayer because of sexual temptation. She had gotten relief from this a year before, and it had made a big difference in her relationship with her husband. For some reason the temptations had returned and she wanted to be set free for good.

"What happened since we prayed about this last year?" I asked. "Do you know what triggered this return?"

"No, it happened gradually. I can remember the freedom from temptation after we prayed last time, but now it is back. It seems worse than before!" Cathy explained.

"Did God ask you to do anything last time?"

42

"Yes," she said softly, without offering any more information.

"And did you?"

"No," she replied. A look of understanding came over her face, and she continued: "He told me to get rid of some old love letters from a former boyfriend. I was in a relationship before I met my husband, but it didn't work out. God told me to get rid of those letters."

"And did He tell you how you should get rid of them?"

"Yes. He was quite specific."

"Are you willing to obey God, as if your life depended upon it?"

"Yes. I know exactly what I need to do, and I know that I will be set free from these temptations as soon as I do it."

Cathy sent a message the next day describing how she burned the old love letters. In the note she expressed the peace and joy she felt as she obeyed. Her faith was restored and she believed her healing was complete.

A few months later I happened to see Cathy at a function. She came up to me with a big smile and shared a little about how much her life had changed because of the freedom God gave her. Her obedience was the right answer to the faith challenge. It was as if Jesus had told her that her faith had made her well.

Chapter Three:
Activate Your Faith

What good is it, my brothers, if someone says he has faith but does not have works? Can that faith save him? - James 2:14

It is one thing to think you have faith, and it is another to act on that faith to make it real. As we saw in the previous chapter, James used the word "works" to describe a step of faith. As intercessors we have opportunity to help others activate their faith.

The Role of Witness

The ninth commandment says "you shall not bear false witness." In every part of your life you should represent the truth, whether in word or deed. Faith, as it is used in this book, is a verb that means to believe the truth. That is why the intercessor bears witness to the truth.

The person who needs prayer may struggle with unbelief or a lack of faith for any of a number of reasons. They may fall prey to a lie that the evil one is using to hold them captive to fear or shame. They may have been influenced by false doctrine or bad theology that distorts the character and nature of God. They may not be able to hear the truth due to a broken spirit and cruel bondage.

We are not required to defend the truth. God's truth needs no defense because it stands on its own merits. We are, however, given opportunities to testify to the truth. In other words, we counteract conditions of unbelief with the gospel, which is the good news about God and His ways.

Learn from Me

Lend Faith

"Always be prepared to make a defense to anyone who asks you for a reason for the hope *(faith)* that is in you (1 Peter 3:15)." Sometimes a person can believe by borrowing from your faith. You may share it with them through instruction or encouragement, but it may also be transferred simply by your presence.

— Learn from Me —

Daniel asked for help with his anger issues. He had a very chaotic childhood and was filled with bitterness toward those who had abandoned him and those who had hurt him. He was out of control, but he was also out of ideas of how to manage the emotional pain.

"Would you be willing to forgive those who hurt you?" I asked.

"I can't," he stated firmly.

"Oh, in fact you can," I explained. "You hold the offense against them, and it is yours to do with as you please. Whether you hang onto it or let it go is completely up to you. No one can force you to forgive, and no one can keep you from forgiving. It's your call. What would you like to do with those offenses?"

He had a look of astonishment on his face. It was obvious that he had never thought about it like this before. He had kept track of these debts for a long time and knew the toll it had taken on his body and emotions. For the first time in his life he had a glimmer of hope, a seed of faith, that he could be set free from it.

With tear-filled eyes he admitted: "I don't know how. Can you help me?"

That was all it took. Just like the father who asked Jesus to help in his unbelief, Daniel was willing to follow my lead by borrowing from my faith.

Articulate a Confession

When a person recalls their earliest memory, it will usually be an event that occurred when they were three or four years old. Prior to age three a child is considered pre-verbal, and research has shown that our memory recall is tied to the ability to express it. That does not mean that children have no memory of things that have happened prior to this time, it just means that it is not as readily recalled.

This same principle affects people's ability to express an emotion. For instance, if they were raised in an environment that was hostile to the expression of emotion they lack the words to describe how they feel. It is as if they are pre-verbal in this area. Once they are given the words, or labels, they quickly express the formerly latent emotions, sometimes with dramatic effect.

— Learn from Me —

I remember praying with a man that fit this description. In his childhood home it was unsafe to express any emotion that was deemed as weak or inferior, while anything that was domineering or controlling was acceptable. God was faithful to renew his mind by replacing thoughts and feelings of hatred and fear with peace and joy. However, when I asked him if he could confirm the change, he was at a loss for words.

He could not describe the inner peace and therefore had trouble believing that the supernatural exchange had taken place. I became a witness for his emotions.

"How does that feel?" I asked.

"I don't know. I'm not really feeling anything," he answered.

"Check for me in that place where your anger usually sits, does it feel any different there?"

"Yeah, it does feel a little different. Like the anger is quiet."

"And, does it feel calm? Like you don't have to keep a lid on it so it won't explode, but it's OK just being there?" I probed.

"Yes!" he exclaimed. "I guess I'm so used to keeping it in check it never occurred to me that it doesn't have to be controlled."

"Right in that place, where it is calm, does it feel comfortable, like it's warm and friendly?"

"Yes! How did you know that?" he wondered.

"That's what peace feels like," I answered.

Notice that in this conversation I did not put any emotions inside this man, but I gave expression to what I knew by faith God had put there in place of his anger. He quickly got in touch with his emotions once he had the words to express them. There was no longer any doubt in his heart that God had made the exchange. His faith had been activated.

— *Learn from Me* —

A similar situation arose in one of our School of Prayer classes. Jenny, a young lady, had been facilitating a prayer session with Naomi, an older woman. Through prayer, Naomi discovered deep seated offenses she carried against her mother. Jenny helped her take an account of the offenses and asked if she would be willing to forgive her mother.

Naomi agreed, and with Jenny acting as witness, began to pray: "Lord, You know my mother didn't do things right. Although she did her best, she didn't really help me grow up right. So, I forgive her for that. Amen."

Jenny followed up by praying: "Lord, I stand as witness to this spiritual transaction where Naomi has chosen to forgive her mother for the offenses she has identified. She forgives her for failing to provide nurture, for not providing proper protection, for being unable to help Naomi discover her true identity in Christ, for allowing her to be placed in harm's way, and for abandoning her as she became an adult. Naomi has released all these offenses of her own free will and we agree that she has forgiven her mother in all these matters. Amen."

"Yes, Lord. I agree with what Jenny said! Amen." Naomi responded. Then she said: "Wow, I just forgave my mother for a lot, didn't I? Thank you for being able to put it into words for me. I feel like all the weight of carrying this around has been lifted off of me."

Jenny helped Naomi activate her faith by expressing the truth in a way that Naomi's experience and spiritual maturity were not able to do. When two or more agree in Jesus' name there is unity in prayer (Matthew 18:19). This is a great example of using the role of witness to help someone articulate their confession or petition.

Confirm Spiritual Transactions

In your Law it is written that the testimony of two people is true. - John 8:17

Jesus taught about the word of the kingdom using the parable of the seeds and different soils. He described the seeds that fell on the path as the word of the kingdom; but the evil one comes and snatches away what has been sown in the heart (Matthew 13:19). This happens to the one who does not understand the word so it does not take root.

The role of the witness is to confirm the meaning of the spiritual transaction to establish truth before the evil one can steal it. This is especially necessary with young believers or the immature in the faith because they are the most susceptible to the wiles of the enemy who would replace the truth with a lie.

I led a man in a spiritual transaction to forgive a former business partner who had betrayed him. We took account of the offenses, which were many, and identified the cost of this betrayal in his life, which was substantial. The pain had been constant for nearly twenty years, but at my invitation he chose to forgive. He felt the freedom that comes from releasing such a large debt.

"You have forgiven your former business partner, and all of the pain of betrayal is now behind you," I confirmed.

"Can it be that simple?" he asked.

"It's that simple. It is a spiritual transaction that has been completed."

"How often will I have to go through this process of forgiving him? After all these years, it's hard to imagine that it will just be gone."

"I'm your witness to this transaction," I said. "If you ever wonder if the forgiveness is complete, you have the right to ask me. I will tell you: 'I was there when you did it, it's a done deal!' It is that simple, and it is that profound."

There have been a few times that this offer has been invoked. One man struggled with his faith and called me for reinforcement, which I gladly provided over the phone. His faith was rekindled immediately.

On another occasion, a man shared that he continued to struggle with temptations related to the issue we had prayed through a year before.

"What?!?" I asked. "I was there when you were set free from that. How could anyone convince you to pick it up again?"

He immediately agreed. My testimony sparked a memory in him and he suddenly felt the same peace he had experienced during our previous prayer time. I encouraged him to hold his peace and not let the evil one snatch the word of truth from him in a moment of weakness. He was very grateful.

> Jesus answered, "Even if I do bear witness about Myself, My testimony is true, for I know where I came from and where I am going, but you do not know where I come from or where I am going." - John 8:14

Jesus made a very important point about the testimony of two or more witnesses in His exchange with the Pharisees in the eighth chapter of John. Jesus is able to bear witness about Himself because He came from the Trinity and returned to the Trinity. Jesus, the Father, and the Holy Spirit all bear witness at once.

When we confess our sin to God the Father, we know that He is sufficient to be witness to the spiritual transaction because He includes the Son and Spirit. I encourage people to engage in spiritual transactions "with God as my witness" because that is more than enough to establish truth.

However, there are also benefits to confessing your sins one to another (James 5:16) and acting as witnesses for each other. It brings the truth into the physical realm in a tangible way and helps activate faith.

Spiritual Transactions

A spiritual transaction is an uncoerced agreement between two willing parties in the presence of two or more witnesses. It is binding in the spiritual, emotional and physical realms. The party of the first part is God; you are the party of the second part; the witnesses are the Son and Holy Spirit (John 8:17-18).

Spiritual transactions put faith into action by intentionally uniting three realms: spiritual, emotional, and physical. When a spiritual concept is acted out in the physical realm it becomes more tangible, and it gives expression in the emotional realm as well.

For example, a petition is a prayer between the asker and his Heavenly Father. It occurs in the spiritual realm and may be invisible to others. I remember talking to my mom about a problem when I was five or six years old. She listened carefully to me and then asked if I had prayed about it.

I was not sure how to answer. I had thought about it, but had I prayed? I had not prayed aloud, but maybe I had prayed in my heart. What would have made it a prayer rather than a thought? Did I say "Amen" after thinking it? Did I close my eyes or fold my hands? If I started praying and got distracted would it still count?

My mom recognized my conundrum by the hesitation to answer and said: "Let's pray together about it right now, okay?"

We prayed. As was my custom, I folded my hands, bowed my head and closed my eyes. I prayed in a conversational but reverent tone and signaled the end by saying "For Jesus' sake, Amen." My mom prayed after, in a very similar manner, though her words flowed smoothly and expressed great love and faith.

This was a spiritual transaction. The words spoken into the spiritual realm between me and my Heavenly Father were also spoken into the physical realm. My humble attitude was expressed by my body, and my mind and heart were joined into the process. It was a very real prayer, and I have Jesus, the Holy Spirit, and my mom as witnesses to prove it.

We know by faith that a prayer of petition is effective in the spiritual realm. We know by action that it is effective in the physical realm. We know by how it makes us feel that it is effective in the emotional realm. A spiritual transaction intentionally integrates and unites all three realms.

Do not be misled by the apparent simplicity of the process. The "sinner's prayer" is a simple act for a person, yet it has eternal consequences. Similarly, spiritual transactions are an expression of supernatural power.

— Learn from Me —

Jon was a young man in need of prayer, so we began our time by asking the Lord to identify the issue to bring to Him in prayer. I opened my eyes to see a look of discouragement on Jon's face. I knew God had revealed something.

"God told me to forgive my father," Jon sighed when I asked.

"That's a great idea," I offered. "Have you taken an account of his offenses that you need to forgive?"

"You don't understand. God told me to forgive him three years ago. I've been praying forgiveness every day since then, but it still doesn't feel like I've forgiven him. I've asked God to help me, and I've tried to forgive in many different ways, but the offense is still there after I pray."

He was reluctant when I asked if he would be willing to walk through the process with me, nor could I blame him. If he really had forgiven every day for three years, he would have tried over a thousand times already.

"I'm not telling you what to do, but I am inviting you to forgive your dad as a spiritual transaction," I explained. "If you are willing, I will ask you to confess aloud to God the offenses you hold against your dad. I will listen and act as a witness. God will be the first witness, and I will be the second witness, and then we can declare the forgiveness to be complete in the spiritual realm by the testimony of two or more witnesses. Okay?"

He was willing and bowed his head to pray. The confession was substantial, which is no surprise because of the number of times he had rehearsed it. His heart was solemn and sincere as he chose to release his father from all of those offenses. I followed him in prayer as a witness and declared the forgiveness to be complete.

Jon's eyes popped open after the prayer, and he looked totally surprised.

"I just forgave my father!" he exclaimed. "Wow, it's really done. I don't have any ill-feelings toward him, the bitterness is gone, and there is no judgment in my heart against him!"

"Check into that place in your heart where you felt the offense before and let me know if you find any trace of it left."

"It's totally gone! I can remember when I would be so mad at him I couldn't talk. But as I think about that now, it's almost as if I don't remember what being mad feels like. This is unbelievable!"

He tested his heart and emotions to see if there were any other offenses lurking, but they had all been forgiven. He was at complete peace in his spirit and soul.

Then he asked me the question I expected: "Okay, why was I able to forgive my father this morning, when I've been praying to forgive him every morning for three years and it hasn't happened? What's different?"

I shared with him about the power of doing things God's way, and how we have noticed the effectiveness of following His commandments, precepts and suggestions. Jesus said:

In your Law it is written that the testimony of two people is true. - John 8:17

A spiritual transaction combines God's promises and laws to establish truth in the spiritual, emotional and physical realms. Jon experienced the supernatural power of God to forgive his father, and the devil could not snatch that truth away because we had invoked the law of witnesses.

There are several situations where we have found a spiritual transaction to be especially powerful when interceding with someone. Here are some examples and scripts we incorporate into our prayer times.

Prayer of Confession

The Holy Spirit convicts of sin and the sinner is given the opportunity to admit his failure and receive forgiveness, a full pardon, from God. There is no way to pay back the debt of the mistake, and there is no way to justify it in part or whole. The only way to erase the debt and settle the score is to receive forgiveness.

Jesus died on the cross and His death paid the penalty for sin. All sin. Every sin that has been committed, whether someone admits it or not, is covered by His blood. What a shame that some refuse this gift and demand to bear the guilt and shame of their sin.

The prayer of confession is a step of faith through which a sinner acknowledges the need for forgiveness and their willingness to accept it as a gift. The first step of being forgiven is to take an account of the offenses against God. Then we recognize and humbly admit that we are unable to repay the debt. We ask for forgiveness and then experience the freedom from guilt and shame.

Here is a sample prayer:

Confessor:

> *Lord, I confess that I (list offenses) and that these offenses are sin against You. I am sorry and ask You to forgive me from these sins. Amen.*

Witness:

> *Lord, I stand as witness to this spiritual transaction: that (name) has confessed these offenses and asked for Your mercy and forgiveness. I declare by Your promise that You forgive him from this sin and cleanse him from all unrighteousness in this matter. Amen.*

Prayer of Release

We are created in God's image and have a sense of justice, so when someone does wrong to us it is normal to pick up an offense. Since the person is unable to repay for the offense they caused, we are trapped with the responsibility to hold them accountable. Notice the eternal nature of the conflict: they can never repay and we are forever responsible. The only solution to this trap is to choose to forgive the debt.

The prayer of release is a step of faith by which we choose to forgive offenses done against us. The first step of forgiving is to take an account of those offenses. Then we accept the fact that the one who committed the offense does not have the means to repay the debt. We choose to forgive, then experience freedom from carrying that judgment. Here is a sample prayer:

Forgiver:

> *Lord, I confess that (name) sinned against me with these offenses (list them). I choose, by my own free will, to release (name) from this debt in the past, present and future. As far as I am concerned, (name) owes me nothing in this matter any longer. Amen.*

Learn from Me

Witness:

> *Lord, I stand as witness to this spiritual transaction: that (name) has confessed these offenses done against him by (name). He has chosen to release (name) of these offenses of his own free will, and I declare that he has forgiven from his heart. Amen.*

— Learn from Me —

I prayed with a man who had been raised by a single mom. His biological father had abandoned them before he was born, and his mother was ill-equipped to raise him on her own. He lacked the protection and provision that should have come from his father, and he was cheated out of proper nurture and unconditional love from his mother. He had paid the price for this lack all his life and it showed. I asked if he would be willing to forgive his parents for their failure.

"Oh, I think I already have," he answered. "I mean, for all the things that I've done, who am I to judge? And besides, they probably did the best they could."

I reminded him about the price he had paid because of their inability and then added: "You haven't already forgiven them. What you have attempted to do is justify their sin, to explain away the cost and to lower the standards by comparing it to your sin. Let me ask you, when you think about how you were raised, does your explanation resolve the conflict and leave you with peace?"

"No, certainly not!" he said.

"I'm going to invite you to forgive them, and to do it as a spiritual transaction. If you are willing, you can confess to God the debt they owe you, and then tell Him that you choose to release them from that obligation. After you have finished, then I will pray as witness. Would you like to do this?"

He agreed and let me coach him through his part as Forgiver. I acted as Witness to confirm the release. Then I asked him how he felt.

"Wow, there was a heavy spot in my heart that I didn't even know was there, but it's gone now! I felt the weight just slide right off, and it's like I can breathe easier now," he said. "The conflict is really gone, and now I do feel peace."

The forgiver benefits from the release.

Request for Truth

What we believe to be true is our paradigm. It constitutes our guiding principles which are accumulated from all our former conclusions. Mind renewal leads to transformation as we accept God's truth in place of those convictions. This works best when we interrogate our beliefs and ask the Lord to confirm or replace them.

A belief can be identified by how it makes us feel or act. Then we "take it captive" by calling it out, by stating it as the conviction in our heart. Remember that what we believe in our heart overrides what we believe in our mind. We may need to avoid reasoning and justification that tries to explain away our heart-held conviction. It is the guiding belief in our heart that we must interrogate.

This spiritual transaction is followed with listening prayer, which is an intentional act of asking and allowing God to reveal truth. We can expect God to renew our mind with a new thought, memory, feeling, word, or idea.

> *Lord, I confess that I believed this to be true: (what you believed to be true that caused you to respond in a certain way). I surrender this belief to You and ask You to reveal Your truth to me in this matter.*

Make an Exchange

God initiated a great exchange for us when He accepted our sin and gave us righteousness in its place. This He accomplished through the death of Jesus on the cross. He still offers to make exchanges with us. We can release our sinful thoughts, feelings, actions, and traits and receive His good gifts.

Learn from Me

This spiritual transaction is a way to activate a person's faith as they are engaged in meaningful participation with God's will through prayer.

> *Lord, I confess that I have misused your gift to me. I have been (state your unredeemed trait, such as stubborn, critical, or angry.) I ask You to redeem this trait and exchange it for (state the redeemed trait, such as loyal, honest, or passionate.) I surrender my old way and choose to accept Your perfect gift in its place.*

Generational Curse

A family tradition of sin is a clear indication of a generational curse. In fact, anytime one generation is compelled by a sin issue because of the transgressions of the parents it is a signal of a generational influence. This spiritual transaction is most effective when the petitioner knows the nature of the sin committed by the previous generations and is able to forgive specifically.

For instance, a person who expresses anger and physical abuse to others may be reacting in a way he experienced while growing up. The father or mother that abused him in childhood was probably a victim of the same kind of abuse in their childhood. We are able to break off this generational curse with the following spiritual transaction:

> *Lord, I choose to forgive the sins of fathers, grandfathers, and great-grandfathers (list the offenses). I ask that You declare the sin of this curse to be forgiven, that there is no legal ground for it to be passed from this generation to the next, and that this generational curse is now null and void in the sight of God and man. Amen.*

Throughout the book of Deuteronomy, God presents blessings and curses as a choice. It is an either/or proposition because the two are connected. We see God's desires to replace a curse with a blessing. When we have received forgiveness, forgiven our forefathers, and asked God to break off the curse it is appropriate to ask Him for the blessing that takes its place.

Imagine the new family traditions that are started after this kind of exchange!

Authority over Spirits

An evil spirit gains access in a person's life by invitation, manipulation, deception, or through a spiritual legal loophole. It operates its own will in defiance of the person's will, causing sin, rebellion and rejection of God's ways. Once the legal ground is removed the authority of Jesus Christ is able to force it to leave. Christians have that authority invested in them as agents of the Lord. Here is a sample command to cast out an evil spirit:

> *Spirit of fear (anger, rebellion, rejection, etc.), you are not welcome here. I command you to leave in the name of Jesus and never return.*

Rash Oath or Vow

Our covenantal God never breaks His promise or goes back on His word. We are made in His image, and when we make a promise, whether an oath or vow, we are bound to it. God never makes a promise that He cannot keep, but we are not perfect. That is why He says: "If a man vows a vow to the LORD, or swears an oath to bind himself by a pledge, he shall not break his word. He shall do according to all that proceeds out of his mouth (Numbers 30:2)." God is willing to forgive that sin (see Leviticus 5:4-5) but Satan wants to hold us to our unwise promises.

For instance, a boy who was bullied in school grew desperate and made a promise: "I will never let anyone pick on me again!" We discovered this rash oath as we prayed about his inability to trust God to protect him. Satan held him to the promise that he alone was responsible for his protection.

He received forgiveness from God for making this rash promise which he could not keep. Then we broke off the binding nature of its consequences by appealing to a higher authority (see Numbers 30:3-13).

Learn from Me

Here is a sample prayer:

> *Lord God, I am aware that I made a rash promise to myself*
> *(oath) or another (vow) when I swore (state oath or vow). I*
> *choose to appeal to You as the Higher Authority and ask*
> *You to break this oath or vow and declare it null and void.*
> *Amen.*

Break Soul Ties

An intimate relationship creates a union, or a soul tie, between those involved. God established this to fuse a man and woman together into "one flesh" as described in Genesis 2:24. The consummated marriage unites two individuals in the spiritual, emotional and physical realms.

An unholy bond occurs when there is a union outside of marriage. A common example of this is sexual intimacy other than between husband and wife, such as premarital sex or adultery. The Apostle Paul refers to this when he writes: "Or do you not know that he who is joined to a prostitute becomes one body with her? For, as it is written, 'The two will become one flesh' (1 Corinthians 6:16)." Physical intimacy crosses over into the emotional and spiritual realms.

However, breaking this bond creates fragmentation and loss. It is as if part of your heart is torn off by the one leaving, and part of their heart remains attached to you. The end result is that each participant has voids because of what they lost and foreign material because of what remains.

It is not just sexual intimacy that creates an unholy bond. These bonds can happen in the emotional and spiritual realms as well. Emotional and spiritual intimacy happen when we share at a deep level of oneness reserved for marriages. We break off these soul ties with this kind of spiritual transaction:

> *Lord, I confess that I made an unholy bond that united my*
> *soul with (name of person). I ask You to forgive me. I ask*
> *You to restore to me any part of my heart and soul that I*
> *gave away, and I ask You to return to them anything that*
> *I took which was not mine to take. I ask that You break*

*this soul tie and renew my mind with purity in this matter.
Amen.*

These spiritual transactions activate faith. Each one is
designed to comply with spiritual laws by following the rules
and concepts understood from God through His word. They are
activated when they are spoken into the physical realm,
witnessed by the Truth, who is Jesus, and experienced in the
emotional realm through our feelings. All three realms are
engaged as the whole person takes this step of faith.

*Therefore, confess your sins to one another and pray for one
another, that you may be healed. The prayer of a righteous
person has great power as it is working. - James 5:16*

The letter of James is very practical, and this verse addresses
the powerful role of forgiveness in the healing process. It also
indicates the power of public confession. This is a spiritual
transaction that goes hand in hand with praying for one
another. I believe one key benefit of confessing sins to one
another is the activation of faith, and the same is true for
breaking curses, rash vows, and removing soul ties. These are
tools for the righteous person whose prayer has great power.

Courtroom of Heaven

*Let us then with confidence draw near to the throne of
grace, that we may receive mercy and find grace to help in
time of need. - Hebrews 4:16*

We are invited to draw near to the throne of grace with
confidence because Jesus, the Son of God, is our High Priest. I
love the image this calls to mind. Imagine this throne room
with God sitting as the Judge who oversees and makes a ruling
on every spiritual transaction.

There you are, standing trial in front of the throne. While you
know the promise that this is the throne of grace, you are in
awe because it is also the judgment seat. Everything you have
done (Romans 3:23), every careless word spoken (Matthew
12:36), and every thought is exposed before the court.

Learn from Me

On your right-hand side is the prosecuting attorney. He is the one who brought charges against you and accused you of capital offenses. In fact, you are never free from his charges since he is "the accuser of our brothers, who accuses them day and night before our God (Revelation 12:10)." He has knowledge of the law and a reputation as the ultimate legalist. He is also called the devil because he always opposes God.

Next to the judge is a witness, called by the prosecution. This witness, a close friend, is under oath to tell the truth, the whole truth, and nothing but the truth. The prosecution begins to interrogate the witness to prove you committed the sins for which you are standing trial, for every careless word you have spoken, and even your errant thoughts. Nothing is beyond his notice, and he is ruthless.

Your heart sinks. Your friend in the witness stand saw you do those things and heard you say those things. Like it or not, he is an eyewitness and he will be forced to give testimony. You are as good as dead. Guilty as charged.

The case is made by the prosecution and it seems ironclad. The prosecution rests and the Judge turns to the defense. He is Jesus Christ and He will cross examine the witness.

"Were you present when the accused sinned, and did you see him commit the act? Remember, you are under oath."

The witness for the prosecution answers reluctantly. "Yes, I was there and saw him do it."

"Were you present when the accused was forgiven for that sin, and did you see him be released from all obligations for committing that act? Again, remember you are under oath."

"Yes! I was there when he confessed his sin and was forgiven and cleansed from all unrighteousness," answers the witness for the defense, this time with much more enthusiasm.

When you are being accused by the devil, can you imagine this scenario with Jesus coming to your defense? When you are tempted to judge someone else, can you imagine being rescued from being a witness for the prosecution?

For this is the will of My Father, that everyone who looks on the Son and believes in Him should have eternal life, and I will raise him up on the last day." - John 6:40

These are the tools and prayer strategies we use to help people activate their faith. As it says in the verse above, it is the will of God that everyone should look on the Son and believe in Him so they shall receive eternal life. That is the ultimate definition of healing: to have life everlasting. This great promise is accepted by faith, and it is a great privilege to be a witness for this act of grace.

Chapter Four:
Redeemed Traits

If I speak in the tongues of men and of angels, but have not love, I am a noisy gong or a clanging cymbal. - *1 Cor. 13:1*

God designed each person with special character traits that express his or her personality and unique identity. The first hints of what will come are subtle and usually spotted by the closest care givers, such as mother and father. By two or three years of age the traits become more obvious. Extra care is needed at this stage to guide the development of those traits into expressions of love.

For instance, an infant may be described as a "happy" or "responsive" or "temperamental" baby. The core identity then begins to emerge over the next few years and the description may change to "fun loving" or "sensitive" or "willful," respectively. The differentiation continues throughout childhood and into adulthood as each trait is emphasized or suppressed. The mature person finds it easy to be the "life of the party" or "caregiver" or "persuasive" because it comes naturally to them.

Conflict arises when a person acts out of character.

This can happen by external influence, such as when an authority figure redirects them by saying "be serious" or "don't take it personally" or "give it a rest." The growing child may try to check his natural character or force an unnatural response in its place.

A person may also act out of character by an internal influence. They may believe it is unsafe or unwise to appear happy, or compassionate, or strong willed. In such a case they choose to suppress their true identity and respond with a learned behavior instead.

Pain exists wherever a person acts in conflict with the identity they were designed to have. That pain occurs in the spiritual, emotional and physical realms. It points to the source or origin of a problem that needs to be healed.

Survivors of abuse or trauma commonly adopt an identity that promises less risk. For instance, a person may suppress a strong-willed character in favor of a compliant nature if they have experienced personal harm from a battle of wills. However, a lifetime of suppressing one's rights or choosing against one's wishes leads to pain in that person's emotions or body.

In another example a man may believe his only pathway to success is to be self-motivated and driven. He may override his natural happy-go-lucky personality with that of a Type-A hard-charger. While this affected personality change may lead to improved performance in his job, it will silently eat at his personality. To compensate, this kind of person often adopts a "work-hard-play-hard" lifestyle, which is a feeble attempt at resolving the personality conflict.

These examples show what happens when a person exchanges a natural trait for a substitute or suppresses the natural trait altogether. However, a more common conflict comes when a person uses a character trait in an unredeemed way rather than the way God intended.

But Have Not Love

And if I have prophetic powers, and understand all mysteries and all knowledge, and if I have all faith, so as to remove mountains, but have not love, I am nothing. - *1 Corinthians 13:2*

Without love a character trait is unredeemed. It is self-serving and becomes a clanging cymbal or noisy gong, worth nothing. Even great traits, such as prophecy, knowledge, and faith, are worthless when consumed rather than shared.

For instance, the gift of knowledge is a wonderful tool when used for building up the body of Christ. The right information can be made available for the right situation and missing pieces are put in place for the common good. The one to whom knowledge is entrusted can offer it as a gift for the benefit of the community.

However, if a person has great knowledge without love he may become an information hoarder. Rather than sharing information with others for mutual benefit it is meted out as a currency to gain control, or for other selfish purposes. The unredeemed gift puffs him up with pride and gives him a false sense of security. As Paul says, "He is nothing."

The devil's scheme includes hijacking a person's primary character trait to render the redeemed aspect useless and inflame the unredeemed side. Early in our ministry, our prayers to help liberate people ran into resistance when we tried to eradicate the unredeemed trait. Then we learned that the problem is not the trait, but the way in which it is used. Our prayer strategy now is to pray that God redeem the trait rather than eliminate it. We ask God to transform the character trait so it shines through the personality in the way He originally intended.

— Learn from Me —

I grew up in Iowa in the Sixties and Seventies, the eldest of two daughters of a mild-mannered mother and a strong-willed father. I can remember being told on a number of occasions, by a variety of family members, "you are so stubborn, you're just like your father!" Even as I write this many years later, there is no sting in the memory of those words. I admired my dad a great deal, so to me being called stubborn was a compliment!

I was in my mid-twenties, as a slowly maturing Christ-follower, when it began to dawn on me that every time the Lord addressed stubbornness or being "stiff-necked" it was not a compliment. For the first time, I was confronted with enough self-awareness to recognize that the Holy Spirit was convicting me of a character trait that needed to change. One of the problems with stubbornness however, is that according to one dictionary definition it is "difficult to move, remove or cure."

Learn from Me

I began to pray to the Lord with sincere dismay: "Lord, You are telling me that this is an aspect of my personality that You don't approve of, but I *am* stubborn, and I don't have the slightest idea what to do about it!"

Here's the good news and a key to understanding redeemed and unredeemed character traits: The Lord has created our inmost being in a fearful and wonderful way (Psalm 139:13-14) and the Spirit has given each of us spiritual gifts "for the common good ... to each one, just as He determines (1 Corinthians 12:7, 11)." The Lord doesn't expect us to stop being who we are. He wants us to submit to the Holy Spirit to learn how to use the gifts He has given us.

Left to my own devices I operate in stubbornness, which is no gift to me or anyone else. But if I allow the Holy Spirit to teach me how to use or steward my gift as He intends, I function from perseverance. James chapter 1 says that perseverance leads to maturity as we bear the testing and trials that come to each of us in this life.

Stubbornness never improved or edified any of my relationships with the Lord, my husband, children, or anyone else. However, my ability and willingness to persevere, even in the midst of testing, allows me to lean into the Lord's strength rather than my own. As a redeemed trait, my natural tenacity encourages others.

— Learn from Me —

Terry was a sensitive young boy in a strong body. He was the biggest and strongest in his class every school year, beginning in the first grade. He excelled at sports and thrived in the team environment. His father saw great potential and his coaches enthusiastically encouraged him to discover his peak performance.

"Come on, Terry! Hit 'em!" his football coach yelled. "Don't back down. Don't give up. You're stronger and meaner than they are."

Terry wanted to please his coach, his dad, his teammates, and the fans in the stands. He would get psyched up with the team, emoting until he felt the rush of adrenalin that would fuel the next conquest. He believed there was no room for being sensitive and that compassion was a crack through which weakness could creep. He kept his feelings in check and became a hardworking, driven performer.

He won the admiration of others by his performance through high school and college. After his sports career, he took those tools into the workforce and his family life. When things got tough, he reached into that part of his past and found drive and determination. While some were impressed with his accomplishments, most of his relationships suffered under the pressure.

He was torn. The harder he worked at something, the greater the conflict inside. He had anger problems and a tendency to isolate himself. He took on incredible responsibility but shut others out to do so. The stress raised his blood pressure and gave him indigestion. His resentments pushed him into wild emotional swings to the point that he wondered if he was bi-polar. He was at his wit's end.

God revealed the root of the issue as we interrogated the feelings and behaviors in prayer. Terry had suppressed his gift of compassion so completely that he forgot it was there. He had come to believe that the skills of motivation and perseverance were accurate expressions of his personality.

"Lord, I realize that You created me to be sensitive with a gift of compassion," he prayed. "But I have shelved that gift and operated on my own initiative instead. Please forgive me."

Immediately Terry felt a weight lifted from his shoulders and a rush of kindness fill him. His face changed, like he had just discovered a secret.

"Oh! It's OK for me to be sensitive. It's not weakness because I really do care about people," he explained. "I thought I wanted to make them happy, but it's really more like I want what's best for them."

"Yes, that's the gift of compassion at work," I affirmed.

We talked about Bible characters, such as Moses and David, who had compassion and strength, and were examples he could use as guides for operating in his giftedness. He was relieved to let go of his driven persona and accept his true identity. He discovered that he could accomplish more in his work and family by being himself than he ever did by striving.

— Learn from Me —

There is a cliché that a person's greatest strength may also be his greatest weakness. This can happen because each trait has a redeemed or unredeemed expression. As you read through the following examples of traits, pay attention to the adjectives that describe your current personality. Take note if they tend to be in the redeemed or unredeemed side. You may find that some of your traits swing back and forth between the sides. Be encouraged that God can redeem any trait if you are willing.

Faith

Faith is a great strength that enables a person to trust God in all circumstances, to believe the truth without evidence, and to remain steadfast to a position despite great opposition or obstacles.

The redeemed side of faith is assertive, bold, confident, decisive, dependable, optimistic, patient, persistent, reliable, steady, and trustworthy. The unredeemed side is stubborn, belligerent, bossy, dominating, headstrong, opinionated, secretive, and self-justifying.

Leadership

Leadership is a great strength that allows a person to guide others toward a goal and encourage them to participate at their highest and most effective level.

The redeemed side of leadership is assertive, attentive, confident, considerate, decisive, disciplined, helpful, selfless, persistent, and venturous. The unredeemed side is attention-seeking, cold-hearted, domineering, manipulative, insensitive, bossy, impatient, self-important and self-seeking.

Discernment

Discernment is a great strength that helps a person know right from wrong and good from evil. It is a companion gift to leadership and mercy.

The redeemed side of discernment is analytical, careful, confident, decisive, lawful, rational, sensitive, spiritual and straight-forward. The unredeemed side is argumentative, abrasive, bitter, cold-hearted, critical, discriminatory, hostile, distrustful, judgmental, gossiping, insensitive, impatient, intolerant, opinionated and vindictive.

Administration

Administration is a great strength that organizes people and things to reduce risk, maximize productivity, and keep things operating smoothly.

The redeemed side of administration is attentive, careful, controlled, disciplined, industrious, lawful, organized, persistent, realistic, reliable and thoughtful. The unredeemed side is bossy, compulsive, detached, humorless, obsessed, over-cautious, unfriendly, perfectionist, procedural, controlling, rigid, and white-knuckled.

Creativity

Creativity is a great strength that brings new ideas and opportunities to light and discovers solutions to problems.

The redeemed side of creativity is boldness, confidence, cooperative, flexible, helpful, involved, open-minded, optimistic, playful, venturous and willing. The unredeemed side is attention-seeking, careless, disorganized, dramatic, egocentric, flightiness, forgetfulness, grandiose, impatient, impulsive, reckless, undependable, undisciplined, unrealistic and unstable.

Learn from Me

Mercy

Mercy is a great strength that moves a heart with compassion and creates opportunity to demonstrate love to one another.

The redeemed side of mercy is attentive, concerned, gentle, considerate, forgiving, generous, helpful, kind, sensitive, serene, social, thoughtful, and warm. The unredeemed side is codependent, enabling, indulgent, overly-emotional, pitying, submissive, unrealistic, vague, depressive and victimhood.

Giving

Giving is a great strength that directs resources to a place of need and provides the materials necessary for accomplishing a mission.

The redeemed side of giving is attentive, cheerful, concerned, considerate, content, cooperative, dependable, friendly, generous, helpful, humble, industrious, involved, loving, selfless, self-sufficient, sociable, thoughtful and venturous. The unredeemed side is arrogant, attention-seeking, boastful, dominating, gluttonous, greedy, indulgent, controlling, lustful, manipulative, materialistic, self-seeking, snobbish and vain.

Confidence

Confidence is a great strength for leadership and positive influence on others. It helps build faith and engenders loyalty.

The redeemed side of confidence is assertive, decisive, faithful, authoritative, outgoing, optimistic and persistent. The unredeemed side is arrogant, egocentric, lying, preoccupation, self-importance and unrealistic.

Caution

Caution is a great strength for stewardship and is necessary for planning and risk management.

The redeemed side of caution is similar to administration with reliable, modest, and lawful aspects. The unredeemed side of caution is indecision, procrastination, anxiety and fear.

Conversion

There are two keys to converting character traits from their unredeemed to redeemed expressions. First, determine which are true gifts compared to the traits that are affectations. Second, learn to use God-given traits as an act of love rather than for self.

People often deny their true gift because they believe it is wrong to exercise it. Like the tenacious young lady that does not want to be labeled "stubborn" or the sensitive young man that does not want to be called a "sissy," they force themselves to act out of character.

Other people have never learned to steward their character traits as the gifts God has given them. For instance, the confident young lady that acts arrogant and self-important, or the creative young man that is grandiose or flamboyant. They are using their gifts, but not in a loving way. The use of these gifts must be redeemed.

We have learned to ask the question: "What is the redeemed side of this character trait?" Strong and healthy personalities are built around the effective use of God-given traits. We have discovered some interesting ways that character traits can be converted.

Anger to Passion

Know this, my beloved brothers: let every person be quick to hear, slow to speak, slow to anger; for the anger of man does not produce the righteousness of God. - James 1:19-20

The redeemed side of anger is passion.

Anger is a strong emotion that often gives expression to secondary emotions such as fear, betrayal, or rejection. It gives power or emphasis to negative emotions, which is why the epistle of James reminds us that it does not produce the righteousness of God.

Passion is also a strong emotion and gives expression to secondary emotions such as love, agreement, or affection. It adds power or enthusiasm to positive emotions. It is a shame to let the negative emotion of anger dominate over the positive power of passion.

— Learn from Me —

Richard was an angry man and when he lost his temper he was completely out of control. He told me he had never backed down from a fight, even during the many years he spent in prison. He loved his wife but on rare occasions she would be the trigger. The thought that he might hurt her frightened both of them.

When we asked God to reveal the source of Richard's anger he was quickly reminded of the time he fought back against a bully. He was pudgy as a fifth grader, and the frequent object of scorn. He did not have support at home and often failed to do his homework. He performed poorly on tests and was not athletic. All these conditions were fodder for teasing.

One day, out of sheer desperation, he took a swing at the meanest bully. His adrenalin kicked in and he fought like a maniac. The bigger boy was stunned and begged for mercy. Word spread quickly around the school that it was not wise to mess with Richard when he was mad. There was no telling what he might do to you.

That was the day Richard invited a spirit of anger into his life. It seemed like a good idea to an eleven-year-old boy to have a super-power at his disposal for whenever he was threatened. As he grew up, he continued to rely on the unpredictable nature of that spirit of anger.

"Thirty years ago, you invited the spirit of anger into your life," I explained to Richard. "Would you be willing to confess that as sin and ask God to forgive you?"

I led Richard in a prayer of confession and he felt the weight of his sin lift from his chest. I followed up by commanding the spirit of anger to leave him, in the name of Jesus, and never return.

Richard was set free from anger that day. He felt peace wash over him as he was forgiven and it filled him as the anger left. He wondered if a change this dramatic would last.

"Richard, how have you controlled your temper in the past?" I asked.

"Well, I have to guard my feelings," he replied. "If I let myself get mad, then I'm out of control. I have to make sure I don't even start to get mad."

"That's the way it used to be," I assured him. "It's different now that the spirit of anger is gone."

I went on to explain that he was suppressing all of his emotions in an effort to control his anger, and that kept him from feeling joy, love, happiness and contentment. Now that he was free from anger he could dare to experience these positive emotions.

Richard was beaming when I saw him at a gathering a few months later. He introduced me to his wife and she gave me a super-tight hug.

"Thank you for praying with Richard!" she exclaimed. "I have my real husband now."

She went on to describe some of the changes in his life and in their relationship. He had become a passionate man with a zest for life. His enthusiasm was infectious and he had recently been promoted to a position of leadership at work. He cared deeply about things at work, home and church, and was admired for his inner strength and power.

Anger is triggered for self-defense and amplifies fear, shame, control, and a host of other unpleasant emotions. Passion is the redeemed side of anger. It is triggered on behalf of others and gives power or expression to love, unity, affection, and a host of other positive emotions. It acts as a motivator and guide for loving God and one another, which fulfills the commandments.

Depression to Compassion

When He went ashore he saw a great crowd, and He had compassion on them and healed their sick. - *Matthew 14:14*

Compassion is a mixture of sorrow and pity that comes in response to suffering. Jesus saw the effect of sin on a crowd of people and was moved to compassion. He responded by healing their sick. Moses was moved to compassion when he saw the shepherds drive off the seven daughters of the priest of Midian. He responded by rescuing them and watering their flock. Compassion is a powerful emotion that prompts action for others because of their suffering.

Depression is sorrow and pity triggered by personal suffering. As we saw in the preceding section, anger is an expressive emotion that can have companion emotions. Depression, in contrast, is a consuming emotion that absorbs companion emotions. Therefore, depression is a powerful emotion with its own appetite for sorrow.

Elijah suffered persecution at the hands of Ahab and Jezebel and became depressed as evidenced by his wish to die, his withdrawal from others, and his complaints to God (1 Kings 19:1-7). His sorrow and pity were self-reflecting which magnified his suffering. The Lord God intervened to break the vicious cycle.

— Learn from Me —

Allison came to me by referral for help with depression. She characterized herself as an outsider in her own family of origin, whom she described as self-confident to the point of being controlling. She had always felt as though she didn't belong, and now she struggled to maintain boundaries to keep them from causing more pain.

We asked God to reveal the source of the depression, and in response she described being called "too sensitive" and "a drama queen." She said she realized that she always took things too much to heart but didn't know how to stop feeling the way she did.

What a conundrum for Allison. She couldn't help the way she felt and was not accepted by her family for being the "way she was." She was convinced there was something fundamentally wrong with her personality because she was so different from the rest of her family.

Her biggest challenge was not that she felt unacceptable by her family but that she did not feel acceptable to herself. It was a cause of great internal conflict and she was desperate for change. She did not know how to change and somewhere within she even wondered if she deserved to be loved.

We went to prayer to interrogate the belief that she was too sensitive and a drama queen. I invited her to simply ask God.

"Lord, why am I too sensitive? Why have I always been such a drama queen?" Then after a pause she asked, "Lord, am I too sensitive?"

She smiled and then shared, "He said I'm not too sensitive. I'm just sensitive enough! He made me this way." Then she prayed again, "Lord, why did You make me this way?"

Allison heard from God that He had given her a powerful gift of compassion. She was greatly encouraged by this news. It was not wrong for her to feel sorrow or pity in response to suffering but she needed to use it as motivation for loving others.

The gift of compassion must be stewarded appropriately. If it does not prompt you to love others, the sorrow and pity accumulate without a purposeful outlet. On the other hand, you can be tempted to withdraw from others to avoid becoming overwhelmed by their trouble and pain. Allison had chosen the latter.

Compassion must be others-focused if it is to "bear one another's burdens, and so fulfill the law of Christ (Galatians 6:2)." True burden bearing does not transfer suffering from one to another but comes alongside to help carry it. Burden shifting, on the other hand, is an unhealthy transfer of suffering from one to another. Similarly, to take responsibility to prevent another's suffering is also a form of transfer, and we are not called to carry this burden alone. The loving thing to do is to come alongside but not to take over. The law of Christ is to love one another (John 13:34).

When compassion focuses inward, the sorrow and pity become overwhelming. This leads to depression; a vicious cycle of sadness and darkness.

Allison was relieved to discover that her sensitivity was not wrong, but a gift that God gave her for the good of others. She no longer had to quell her sensitivity in a vain attempt to be acceptable to others. She was no longer compelled to fix others' problems or take on their suffering. She was free to express the emotions that came to her when she saw suffering, and in love she drew from her own resources to make a difference. She experienced complete freedom in being her true self.

Compassion is the redeemed side of depression.

The symptoms of depression are sadness and darkness. Many people try to alleviate these unpleasant emotions by turning off their feelings of sorrow and pity. Ironically, to deny these responses is in conflict with their true identity and causes more emotional pain. Then the depression continues to spiral out of control.

The prayer strategy is to accept compassion as a gift for loving others and as a guide for expressing sympathy and empathy in redeemed ways.

Stubborn to Loyal

> But the house of Israel will not be willing to listen to you, for they are not willing to listen to Me: because all the house of Israel have a hard forehead and a stubborn heart.
> - Ezekiel 3:7

The Israelite history is a biblical case study of stubbornness. God called them stiff-necked and hard of forehead because they were unchanging, rebellious and unwilling to listen. A stubborn person is committed to himself and his opinions and is unwilling to submit to others.

A man of many companions may come to ruin, but there is a friend who sticks closer than a brother. - Proverbs 18:24

Loyalty is a character trait used to describe commitment as from a dear friend. The loyal person is unwilling to listen to false testimony and is unchanging in his relationship with his friend.

Both stubbornness and loyalty are characterized by tenacity but they differ depending on the object of commitment. For example, I am stubborn when I am committed to me, but I am loyal when I am committed to you.

— Learn from Me —

Ben was a successful salesman who earned the respect of customers and competitors alike. He was known as a hard worker and always kept his promises, but he had a reputation for being argumentative. He came for prayer because of stress-related health issues due to his driven nature. He had tried to back off the throttle a little bit, but he could never attain a healthy balance.

We began our prayer time by asking God to take us to the place that needed to be healed. Ben was surprised to hear that stubbornness was at the root of his stress. He had never really thought of himself as stubborn, but when God revealed it there was a ring of truth.

"Lord, would you show Ben what is at the root of this stubbornness? When did he become so driven?" I prayed.

Ben remembered when his dad and mom fought a lot and then got separated. It was about a year before their divorce, when he was ten. Ben was determined not to be a bother or make matters worse, and he certainly would not take sides. However, his best efforts to hold the family together were not enough. He was heart-broken and felt like a failure.

"Lord, would you show Ben what he believed to be true during that time?" I prayed.

"I thought there might be something I could do," he said. "I hated to see them fight, especially when I found myself in the middle of their squabbles. They didn't want to hurt me, but neither wanted me either. They argued about who should pay and how much. I believed I could take care of myself, so that's what I started to do."

I took that belief to prayer: "Lord, Ben believed as a ten-year-old that he was responsible for himself and his parents. What do You want to reveal to him about this belief?"

Ben realized at that moment what a huge responsibility he had taken on, a weight much too great for a child that age. He was sad for his parents as he thought back over that time, but also for his loss of childhood. He explained how that same feeling of responsibility and hopelessness fueled his stubbornness ever since. He forgave his parents, accepted forgiveness for taking on their responsibility, and felt a huge relief inside.

I pointed out to Ben that he had tried to operate in the redeemed expression of his gift by being loyal to each parent, proven by his commitment to not take sides. The trauma of divorce and loss of relationship had flipped him into the unredeemed expression of stubbornness. Now that he had forgiven his parents, he was free from defending their choices. He could be loyal to the truth and leave the responsibility of the consequences to God.

Judgment to Discernment

> And it is my prayer that your love may abound more and more, with knowledge and all discernment, so that you may approve what is excellent, and so be pure and blameless for the day of Christ. - Philippians 1:9-10

The redeemed side of judgment is discernment which is a spiritual gift for knowing right from wrong and godly from ungodly. Discernment is awareness of wrong while seeking what is holy and true. The ministry of reconciliation that God calls us to is driven by discernment's focus on the redemptive power of truth. That is why the Apostle Paul states in

Philippians 1:9-10 that love abounds when discernment approves what is excellent, pure and blameless.

Judgment comes from the original sin, which occurred when Adam and Eve ate from the fruit of the Tree of Knowledge of Good and Evil and took responsibility to make the determination. Disgust, or moral hypervigilance, can lead to judgment, as stated in the previous chapter. Legalism and law-based relating operate on black and white interpretations of right and wrong and can also lead to judgment. In fact, the judgmental person searches for failure, makes accusations, and condemns both sin and sinner.

The problem of judgment is not in how it assesses good and evil, but in how it acts on that assessment. Since judgment is devoid of hope it foresees only failure. Little benefit comes from pointing out flaws and failure unless a solution is also offered. Judgment and condemnation are obstacles to loving one another.

— Learn from Me —

Heidi had trouble with trust and forgiveness. Her marriage of seventeen years ended in divorce because of her suspicious nature and insecurity. She found fault with everyone and realized that tendency destroyed relationships. She had been sexually abused as a young girl but had learned to survive. Her main prayer concern was to restore her ability to trust people.

When we asked God for a starting point, Heidi quickly realized that the topic would be her grandfather. She was surprised and disappointed about this because she thought she had dealt with this part of her past. She acknowledged that he had been one of her abusers, so I asked if she had forgiven him.

"Oh, I must have! I never really think about it anymore. Besides, he's dead and I'll never have to see him because he is where he belongs. People like that belong in hell," she said.

"Do you hope he is in hell?" I asked. "Because if you do, it's an indication that you haven't forgiven him."

That shocked her, but as she thought about it she realized it was true. She was still judging and condemning him for what he had done. The pain of her past put her in the role of judge, and she felt responsible to hold him to account for his sin. She felt like the only one who could set the record straight and she wanted to protect other innocent people from becoming victims to such horrific sins. She could see the signs of sexual sin on people and felt equipped by her experience to identify guilty parties.

However, she did not want to be stuck in the role of judge or as a witness for the prosecution. It was obvious that she had not been able to trust others because of this position she had taken. She agreed to follow the steps to forgive her grandfather and others who had harmed her.

Heidi was set free from a spirit of judgment when she forgave her grandfather, and she hoped he was at peace. Suddenly her heart was filled with compassion toward people stuck in sexual sin. She wondered how to rescue them by the grace of God rather than condemn them to hell.

Judgment always leads to condemnation, but discernment is an important tool for the ministry of reconciliation.

Critical to Honest

> *Let no corrupting talk come out of your mouths, but only such as is good for building up, as fits the occasion, that it may give grace to those who hear.* - *Ephesians 4:29*

Critical people are quick to find fault. They often take pride in their opinions and wield their knowledge of good and evil as if it were a helpful tool rather than fruit from a tree of sin. They may be guided by a critical spirit who is preoccupied with evil and failure. They may express their opinion with a critical tongue which verbalizes judgment. What comes out of their mouth is corrupting talk that tears down. They may believe that reserving their harshest criticism for themselves mitigates the damage, but it does not.

*The good person out of the good treasure of his heart
produces good, and the evil person out of his evil treasure
produces evil, for out of the abundance of the heart his
mouth speaks. · Luke 6:45*

The critical person pays attention to detail, but treasures evil
in his heart by identifying and collecting examples of failure
and fault. However, he stores up good treasure in his heart
when he learns to pay attention to detail and focus on the good
instead of the bad. The error is not in the tendency to pay
attention to detail but in the kind of detail that is savored.

A critical spirit, like other traits, can be passed down from one
generation to another as a generational curse. The prayer
strategy is to break the curse and command the critical spirit
to leave. The person is then freed up to exercise his attention
to detail for the benefit of others.

— Learn from Me —

Melissa came for prayer because of problems in her
relationships with her husband and children. She had been
confronted about her harsh words and criticism, but felt she
was being "honest" with her family. She could not understand
why they felt disrespected and belittled. She agreed that the
home had become a hostile environment but blamed her family
for being weak and overly-sensitive.

As we prayed together, Melissa realized that she was repeating
a way of relating that she had experienced from her own
mother. Harsh words and constant criticism were spoken, with
the caveat that this was said "for your own good." She teared
up as she remembered the sting of the disparaging words from
her childhood. She had grown up hearing a litany of mean and
cruel things. Despite how her mother had couched it, having
all her failures pointed out had not turned out for her own good.

"This is a generational thing, isn't it?" she asked. "I remember
how my grandma used to snipe at my mom all the time, too. It
seems like the women in our family compete with each other to
be the first to speak criticism."

Learn from Me

We talked a little more about the damage caused by a critical tongue and took an account of all the ways her life had been affected by it. Melissa was eager to forgive her mom and grandma for passing along the critical spirit, and then she asked for forgiveness for accepting it as part of her personality.

We prayed again and Melissa asked for forgiveness while I acted as her witness. She felt something move in her heart and she smiled as she considered what God had just done in her.

I shared with her a scripture that came to my mind as we prayed:

> The Lord GOD has given me the tongue of those who are taught, that I may know how to sustain with a word him who is weary. Morning by morning He awakens; He awakens my ear to hear as those who are taught. - Isaiah 50:4

I explained that this "instructed tongue" is given to replace the critical one. Now she would be able to speak words that sustain the weary just as quickly as she had formerly been able to blurt out someone's faults.

A week later I received a message from Melissa. She shared that as she was driving home from our appointment God was already giving her words to say to bless her husband. She could not wait to share the good news with him. He was overwhelmed and it completely changed the dynamic of their relationship. He stopped hiding from his wife to protect himself, and instead began showing great faith and confidence in God.

"I've memorized that verse you gave me. Every morning I wake up and ask God to tell me what to say to people to sustain them. Sometimes He gives me words and I have to wait to find out who they are for, and sometimes He reminds me of a person and I have to think about what they need to hear. It has changed all of my relationships!"

Unyielding to Faithful

> *Five times I received at the hands of the Jews the forty lashes less one. Three times I was beaten with rods. Once I was stoned. Three times I was shipwrecked; a night and a day I was adrift at sea; on frequent journeys, in danger from rivers, danger from robbers, danger from my own people, danger from Gentiles, danger in the city, danger in the wilderness, danger at sea, danger from false brothers; in toil and hardship, through many a sleepless night, in hunger and thirst, often without food, in cold and exposure. And, apart from other things, there is the daily pressure on me of my anxiety for all the churches. - 2 Corinthians 11:24-28*

The Apostle Paul is one of the great examples of conversion from unyielding to faithful. When he was still Saul, a devout Pharisee, he was unyielding in his attack against The Way. Nothing could stop him from persecuting Christians because he was completely dedicated to his doctrine. God exchanged Saul's unyielding character for Paul's unwavering faith.

The object of dedication is what distinguishes between the two. An unyielding person is self-centered and does not accept challenges to their mind, will and emotions. In contrast, a faithful person is dedicated to God and His will. Nothing can stop the faithful person's confidence in God's character, promises, purposes, and ways.

Unhealthy Striving to Industrious

> *"Cease striving and know that I am God. I will be exalted among the nations, I will be exalted in the earth." Psalm 46:10*

Unhealthy striving is characterized by placing so much focus on doing, or action, that it puts one's health, emotions, and relationships in danger. The striver is preoccupied with the next obligation and measures everything by performance. Striving can be motivated by fear or insecurity. I heard one man declare that he works hard to keep bad things from happening to him. I heard another man admit that he works hard so that when bad things happen he can say that he did everything he could.

The Psalmist commands us to cease striving. For those who have a lifetime of experience with it, that is easier said than done. Fortunately, the verse goes on to say "and know that I am God." Both an explanation and a promise are given. The explanation is that we can cease striving because "I am God," and by inference, we are not. The promise is that when we cease striving we will know that He is God, and by inference, He will prove it.

— *Learn from Me* —

David was a self-described workaholic. He had heard me teach about the orphan mentality and felt convicted that he had taken responsibility to protect and provide for himself. He had come for clarification, and to argue that working hard was not sin.

Rather than argue, I invited him to a time of prayer. When he agreed, I began our prayer time by asking God to reveal the source of David's motivation and what drives him.

"My dad taught me that a real man works hard," he answered. "And he taught me with a belt. There was no shirking duty or room for laziness in our household."

"And what drives you?" I asked. "What you shared about your dad is how you learned to work hard, but what keeps you at it now? You're certainly not motivated by fear of harsh discipline anymore, right?"

He thought about that for a moment, and then said: "I guess I believe that you have to do your part. It's just something that's true in life. You have to work hard to prove yourself."

We talked a little bit about identity and the fact that you are not just a product of what you do, but who you are. "Your identity," I explained, "is subject to termination if it is defined by a role. When that role is finished, so is your identity."

"Well then, I guess I'll just quit and go on the dole like every other lazy person," he suggested with a defiant tone.

"You are struggling with unhealthy striving," I said. "The opposite of unhealthy striving is not quitting but giving 'healthy effort.'"

As we continued to talk and pray, God showed him that he equated hard work with worth and was still trying to prove himself by his efforts. He was trying to control all aspects of his life and it led to unhealthy striving.

I then led him to the verse in Psalm 46 that says: "Cease striving and know that I am God." David read and reread it, emphasizing the part about knowing God. He repented of self-reliance that led to unhealthy striving, and asked God to be ruler in his life. He relinquished the responsibility back to God and felt a huge burden lift.

I recognized David at a fellowship a few months later, and he came toward me with a warm greeting. He shared that his life had been completely changed, and his family noticed immediately. Now he was working hard but enjoying it. He was volunteering at a small-group in his church and felt he still had time to get together with friends.

"The amazing thing is, I'm getting just as much done at work as I ever did. And I'm doing a lot more that I find fun and fulfilling. Once I gave up unhealthy striving, it's as if I was free to work for the fun of it," he told me.

I smiled. God can do so much with us when we learn who He is and stop trying to manage His business in our strength. David was free to work hard and found great enjoyment in it. God had redeemed his unhealthy striving and turned it into industriousness.

Controlling to Powerful

A controlling person may be operating out of fear or pride. Fear arises in those who have experienced rejection or some similar emotional trauma over which they had no control. They respond by attempting to micromanage their lives to prevent trauma from reoccurring. In other cases, pride causes a person to believe no one else is as capable or has as much to offer. They step into a leadership role because they are unable to trust anyone else.

These take-charge people operate out of the strength of their will. They rehearse success to prove that their leadership is vital while overlooking any hint of failure. This bias can cause them to override the will of others, sometimes with the best of intentions.

The temperament and skill set that comes out of the experience of a controller is useful for powerful leadership. The prayer strategy to redeem this trait starts with acknowledging that violating another's free will is abuse. When this abuse has been confessed and forgiven, the person can reclaim decisiveness and the ability to take responsibility as tools for loving others.

— Learn from Me —

Jim was a large man with a big bass voice, and when he walked into a room he took charge. He exuded confidence and expected people to fall in line behind him. It was his way, and he acted no differently at home than he did at work or in church. He was quick to make decisions, take risks, and move forward. He commanded others to follow his lead.

Everyone has the right to exercise his own free will. If one person overrides the free will of another it is abuse. It is physical abuse if he uses physical force, or the threat of it, to make someone do something they do not choose to do. It is emotional abuse if he uses emotions or plays on feelings to sway them. It is spiritual abuse if he uses God, religion, or doctrine as a tool to control.

Jim felt horrible when he realized how abusive he had been. He was quick to ask God for forgiveness and then brainstormed ways he could ask his family and others to forgive him. God showed him that his controlling behavior came out of feeling rejected. He believed that people would accept and respect him when things went well because he was in control.

Jim was set free from rejection when God showed him how much He loved him. He had great experience, training, and aptitude for managing and he began to use those gifts in an entirely different way. People came to appreciate his powerful influence because he could make things happen.

Impulsive to Courageous

Impulsive people act quickly but may be rash, imprudent and lack follow-through. The unredeemed side of this trait is to be impetuous and hasty. They may believe that any action is better than inaction and put their hope in the idea of "failing forward" or experiencing accidental success. They tend to be designers and entrepreneurs but may be poor listeners and resist authority. They appear to operate on instinct, but it is more accurate to say they live in strength of soul. When guided by their mind, will and emotions they can do great harm to themselves and others.

The redeemed side of this trait is proactivity, bravery and responsiveness. When guided by the Spirit, the courageous person is quick to obey. They are good leaders because the plan they follow is from God, and they are quick to take action.

An exchange from impulsive to courageous occurs when the impulsive person surrenders his rights and submits his will to God.

Lazy to Patient

The sluggard buries his hand in the dish; it wears him out to bring it back to his mouth. - Proverbs 26:15

Laziness can be caused by physical factors such as a poorly fueled or oxygenated body. It can also be caused by a lack of creativity or ideas to act upon. The remedies for these factors are obvious. However, the Scriptures are full of warnings to the sluggard who is chronically lazy. Laziness, or sloth, is a sin of omission because it fails to obey the command to take dominion and be fruitful (Genesis 1:22).

Hedonism and purposelessness are two common themes that show up in slothfulness. The hedonist is self-indulgent and his only purpose is for personal benefit. The purposeless person lacks even that motive. Laziness can be overcome by a higher calling, a purpose of loving and serving beyond self.

The redeemed side of this trait is patience. When this person is motivated by a clear calling or purpose he responds with steadiness and determination. The opposite of lazy is not frenetic but patient.

— Learn from Me —

Phil was a young man with no forward motion and no prospects. He had trouble getting out of bed in the morning, and just as much trouble going to bed at night. His parents asked him to meet with me for prayer.

We asked God to reveal the root cause of Phil's condition, and immediately he realized the offense he held against his parents. He felt marginalized and rejected by their life choices because they were hard-working and hard-charging people. He believed he could never measure up to their expectations and felt sad and hopeless.

Phil accepted my invitation to forgive his parents for causing him to believe he was not acceptable, and he reported a warm glow inside as he released the offense. He suddenly realized that his inaction was a direct response to his offense at their "over-action." He confessed that sin of inaction and as he accepted forgiveness a new sense of peace filled him.

"I think I've been so tired because of feeling hopeless," Phil shared. "Those feelings are gone, and I have a new sense of energy because the weight has been lifted."

He was made new from the inside out by that prayer time. At first his parents wondered if anything had actually changed. They could see a new spark in his eyes as he talked about his plans for the future, but he was not following their "Type-A" behavior. Over the next year he reenrolled in school, methodically worked on his courses, and made consistent progress. No class was too hard for him, and no challenge could deter him. Phil patiently discovered and pursued his new purpose.

The Great Exchange

God offers us a great exchange. He gave His Son in exchange for all sin, and He gives us good things in place of the wages of sin. It does not seem fair, but God's objectives go far beyond fairness. He chooses instead to be extravagant toward us because He is filled with unending love.

A person whose mind has not been redeemed by God does not operate from a place of love. In most cases their traits and gifts are used for self rather than for others. A few kind-hearted or well-intentioned people may do things for the common good, but when things get tough human nature pushes us to self-preservation, and they abandon that idea.

The first step in our prayer strategy is to allow God to reconcile us to Himself through Christ. This is a commitment or recommitment to the Lord as Savior which allows us to operate from a position of love. Not only do we become reconciled in spirit and soul, but our gifts and traits can be aligned to God's way. This is the great exchange by which we go from lost to saved.

The next step in our prayer strategy is to recognize the parts of our identity which are not in agreement with God's truth. Each of these can be exchanged for their redeemed counterpart. For instance, our unredeemed response to fear or pain may be unholy or unproductive coping behaviors. We may have unhealthy emotional responses based on faulty conclusions we have drawn. We can present these undesirable and unpleasant traits to God and He will exchange them with good gifts.

We hold on to coping strategies, unpleasant emotions or harmful responses because of offenses. When we choose to release the offenses by extending or receiving forgiveness we are able to receive something pleasant or beneficial in its place.

For example, a simple prayer of exchange for the trait of stubbornness to loyalty may sound something like this:

Lord, I confess that I have been stubborn in holding to my own opinions. I choose to release my stubbornness and ask that you give me loyalty and faith in exchange. Amen.

Chapter Five:
Weapons for Healing

The weapons we fight with are not the weapons of the world. On the contrary, they have divine power to demolish strongholds. We demolish arguments and every pretension that sets itself up against the knowledge of God, and we take captive every thought to make it obedient to Christ. -
2 Corinthians 10:4-5 (NIV)

The world wages war to weaken or destroy an enemy in a battle for control at the expense of others. Weapons of warfare have changed throughout history. The battle between Cain and Abel appears to have been hand-to-hand combat. Biblical history goes on to recount wars with spears, arrows, horses and chariots. More recent history records guns, bombs and missiles as advancements in weaponry and warfare. Improvements in weaponry are measured by their increased ability to steal, kill, and destroy (John 10:10).

The Apostle Paul writes that our warfare is not of the flesh. The weapons of the world are able to kill or subdue the body and are used to control the world in the physical realm. The weapons of our warfare, on the other hand, are not of the world but have divine power.

We wage war in the spiritual realm with spiritual weapons and our victory overflows into the physical and emotional realms as well. We overcome the thief who comes to steal, kill, and destroy and God brings the results: increase instead of theft, life instead of death, and healing rather than destruction. We use our weapons for healing rather than warfare.

Healing prayer is spiritual warfare. It requires divine power because it seeks supernatural results. It accomplishes what is unreasonable to expect according to the limited ways of the world. The supernatural power of God overcomes the spiritual forces of evil and darkness in this world and the next.

We do not war against flesh and blood. We do not war against ideologies, doctrines or religions. We do not war against cultural biases or selfish ambitions. We war against the rulers, authorities and powers of this dark and sinful time. We war against the spiritual forces of evil in the heavenly places.

For instance, the Apostle Paul wrote that the ways of the world are of no value in stopping the indulgence of the flesh. He challenged the believers in Colossae by saying: "Why do you submit to regulations such as 'Do not handle, Do not taste, Do not touch'" according to human precepts and teachings? These have an appearance of wisdom in promoting self-made religion and asceticism and severity to the body, but they are of no value in stopping the indulgence of the flesh. (Colossians 2:20-23, paraphrase mine.)

No matter how hard one tries to refrain from sin by self-made religion, rules and strong will power, true freedom only comes by divine power. The addict, for example, will always be an addict if sobriety is maintained by sheer will power, rules, accountability partners, and other tools of the flesh. But true victory is possible through the supernatural power of God. The one who has been reconciled to God through Christ has become a new creation. He is no longer an addict but is forever free to be the person God created him to be.

We do not wage war according to the flesh. We use these weapons for warfare to storm the gates of hell, and as the forces of evil are expelled, they become weapons for healing.

Prayer strategies are not intended to be recipes or directives that detract from the simple truth that healing happens as we follow the leading of the Holy Spirit. In the next few pages we will consider the terms found in 2 Corinthians 10:4-5 as nomenclature to help frame prayer strategies. I do not believe Apostle Paul's intent was to make distinctions between strongholds, arguments, and pretensions in these verses, but to use these terms as near-synonyms to bring a broader understanding to our spiritual warfare.

In a similar way, he uses many different terms to describe spiritual gifts in Romans, 1 Corinthians, and Ephesians. Some are quite similar, like leadership and administration, while others are distinct, like tongues and prophecy. The terms are not to be treated as items on a menu but general descriptions of ways the Spirit works through people.

Consider the different mental images you get from these terms for spiritual battles but keep your eye on the Holy Spirit for discernment in each divine appointment. You may find that He guides you into a strategy against a "lofty opinion" in one setting that presents as an "argument" in another. Jesus knows how to renew minds, so stay yoked to Him.

Demolish Strongholds

For we do not wrestle against flesh and blood, but against the rulers, against the authorities, against the cosmic powers over this present darkness, against the spiritual forces of evil in the heavenly places. - Ephesians 6:12

A stronghold is another name for the spiritual forces of evil to which Paul refers. It occurs when these forces defend ill-gotten spiritual authority and wield it against the ways of God. A stronghold is a place of power and influence for darkness in a cosmic war between good and evil. When Paul describes them as being in heavenly places he does not mean they are in the presence of God, but that they are other-worldly and not visible in the physical dimension of earth. Yet these other-worldly dominions exert great influence in the physical world through the spiritual realm.

The term stronghold, as used in the Bible, is a word picture of a castle or city with thick walls. As spiritual forces of evil become established in a person, the influence of the stronghold grows, and the stronger it becomes the more heavily it is defended. The forces of darkness are not willing to easily give up an established position. From the well-defended position of the stronghold, rulers, authorities and evil powers continue their mission to steal, kill, and destroy.

Rulers

Rulers are spiritual beings. They are personified in Scripture as demons, devils or spirits but each is an individual with personality, rights, and will. A social structure in the spiritual realm dictates protocols for interaction amongst these spiritual beings based upon their relative power and authority. God has set the limits and regulations for the ways these rulers can interact with human beings.

God granted all created beings the gift of a will, which provides freedom to make choices. God also has a will which He exercises with perfect balance between justice and mercy. Since His nature is love, every choice He makes is loving. Humans have a will that gives them the freedom to act in good or evil ways. Rulers within a stronghold, however, use their God-given will to make evil choices.

"Free will" is the term we use to describe a being's ability to make an uncoerced choice. Each being demonstrates its personality through this channel.

God has the power and authority to override our free will, but He does not because doing so would conflict with His loving nature. It is abuse to override another's free will and love never abuses.

Spiritual forces of evil have not been granted the power or authority to override our free will, but they will do anything they can to manipulate and deceive us into abdicating the authority over our will to them. This abdication gives them the opportunity to abuse us by manipulating our will.

Jesus demonstrated the perfect way we should interact with our Creator when He said, "Thy will be done." He chose to align His will with the Father's even to the point of death on the cross. When we follow His example, we enter into perfect relationship with God because there is no conflict between our will and His. God's gift of free will allows us to make the same choice Jesus did to yield our will to God the Father.

One of the symptoms of a stronghold is the presence of a third will. God's will, like His eternal character, is always present. The person's will is an irrevocable gift from God. The third will belongs to a "ruler" of a stronghold whose will is opposed to the will of God. When we surrender authority to a stronghold, this spiritual being responds and relates to us in an abusive and coercive way, to confuse and distort the truth by bombarding us with accusations, lies, and negative thoughts. It feels like a loss of free will because though we are trying to obey God, there is another spiritual force at work within us.

Paul describes it this way: "For I do not do the good I want, but the evil I do not want is what I keep on doing. Now if I do what I do not want, it is no longer I who do it, but sin that dwells within me (Romans 7:19-21)." The "sin that dwells within" can also be described as a spiritual being with a mind and will of its own.

Authorities

Authority is God's sovereign order of all things. The depth and complexity of His ways are beyond comprehension. The Psalmist attempts to give voice to it by saying that the works of the LORD are great, full of splendor and majesty, and His righteousness endures forever. The works of His hands are faithful and just; all His precepts are trustworthy; they are established forever and ever, to be performed with faithfulness and uprightness (Psalm 111: 2-3, 7-8).

This concept of God's authority is too big for words like order, works, and precepts, so to the extent we are able we develop laws to describe the individual components. For instance, we use laws of nature to articulate parts of God's ordered universe. There are many laws but only one authority.

A stronghold operates according to its "authorities" or laws. We use the plural form of the word to indicate that these are incomplete or distorted expressions of God's true authority.

God is the supreme authority. He establishes and assigns all levels of authority under Him, as He pleases. He granted authority to mankind in the Garden of Eden, for example, when He said to them, "... fill the earth and subdue it, and have dominion over ... every living thing that moves on the earth (Genesis 1:28)."

When Adam and Eve were deceived in the Garden of Eden they sinned and rebelled against God's authority. The "fruit" of their sin was the "knowledge of good and evil," and with that knowledge they wrested the responsibility of evaluating good and evil from God and took matters into their own hands. They detached their God-given authority from under Him and, in an act of defiance, placed their opinion of right and wrong above His.

As in the Garden, our sin transfers the intended alignment of authority away from God's will and into the purposes of the enemy. Ephesians 6:12 uses the term "authorities" for the transferred authority that conflicts with God. A system of rules or laws operates in a stronghold, and the nature of that stronghold is determined by the sin on which the authority is based. A stronghold uses its laws to override a person's will and control their actions.

For instance, sexual sin breaks from God's design and aligns with the sex stronghold (see Chapter Seven). Authority over sexuality, intimacy, and purity are exploited by this stronghold to cause transgressions which increase the influence it exerts. The person who struggles under this stronghold has very little power to escape its consequences.

We often refer to this transfer of authority as "legal ground" which the devil uses to manipulate, control and abuse people. He will take advantage of any legal ground given and will push even further to deceive the unsuspecting into letting him use legal ground he has not been given.

However, we have hope that strongholds can be overcome because we know that sin ultimately has no dominion over us, since we are not under the law but under grace (Romans 6:14).

Cosmic Powers

The "cosmic powers over this present darkness," as described in Ephesians 6:12, are spiritual forces of evil in the heavenly places. Though this power is other-worldly it affects the material world. Cosmic powers are hard to understand from an earthly perspective and impossible to prove with our laws of nature. Scripture gives us some explanation but we also learn by observing the consequences of the power and perceiving its cause.

For instance, a generational curse acts as a cosmic power. We gain insight about this force from the Ten Commandments. God describes Himself by saying "I the LORD your God am a jealous God, visiting the iniquity of the fathers on the children to the third and fourth generation of those who hate Me (Exodus 20:5)." The iniquity, or sinful nature, is passed down to the next generation unless the father repents and submits to the Lord's ways.

A generational curse seems to expand from one generation to the next. For example, alcohol addiction is a coping strategy for conflicts within a stronghold. A father may engage in social drinking while occasionally using it to solve a fear problem. His son becomes a heavy drinker, using it to address additional issues. His grandson becomes firmly addicted to alcohol and loses all control over this behavior. Finally, his great-grandson is born with fetal-alcohol syndrome. As far as I know, this pattern of increasing spiritual forces of evil has not been documented with scientific analysis. But we have seen it played out in countless prayer sessions, and it follows the nature of God by which He gives increase from one generation to the next. His command to be fruitful and multiply was intended for blessing, but this cosmic power applies the expansion principle to curses.

We also learn about cosmic powers through examples recorded in biblical history. The Israelites were commanded to cleanse the Promised Land because it had been used for idol worship. God's curse of the ground (Genesis 3:17) could not be overcome because the people worshipped worthless idols that had no power. Later, the tribes of Israel were at times subjected to the same curse on the ground because of their besetting (chronic) sin of idolatry.

Sabbath rest is also subject to a cosmic power. A blessing exists for those who obey, but consequences for those who ignore the law. This is true for man's work (rest the seventh day), for the land's work (rest the seventh year), and for the national economy (year of jubilee). God rectified the Israelite's disregard for this law by giving the land rest for seventy years during the Babylonian captivity.

Strongholds use cosmic powers to block mankind from God's promised blessings and favor. The authority usurped by the stronghold yields curses rather than blessings because it aligns with the enemies of God. For instance, the Israelites faced famine when they turned to idol worship but received God's blessings and increase each time they repented.

The Holy Spirit gives us insight into the spiritual realm when we seek truth from Him. He can reveal the root cause of a stronghold that has a strangle-hold on a person or group of people.

We attack strongholds to demolish them. The purpose of the attack is to destroy the misaligned authority that resides within and replace it with the authority of the Kingdom of Heaven. We banish the rulers, reconnect authority to God as the highest authority, and revoke the cosmic powers of evil.

Our role is offensive, not defensive. Jesus said that the gates of hell will not prevail or withstand against His church. A stronghold represents a gate of hell, and we are authorized to demolish it.

Destroy Arguments

A person's belief system, or paradigm, can become an "argument" as listed in 2 Corinthians 10:5. What we believe to be true affects our identity and personality. Any belief system that is raised against the knowledge of God is an "argument."

The human nature demands explanation. Consider the three-year-old who constantly asks "Why?" The question, even demand, comes from an urgent desire to know. I believe this innate condition becomes all the more evident as the child gains words to articulate the requests and accept answers.

I love information, reasoning, logic, and wise conclusions. In fact, the spiritual gift of teaching is evidenced by the accurate handling of information and an ability to explain it to others. However, there is a dark side to these "arguments."

Ever since eating fruit from the Tree of Knowledge of Good and Evil, mankind has been preoccupied with knowledge and the responsibility for judging good and evil. The combination of knowledge and responsibility drives our demand for explanation. In the absence of an explanation from God, we are willing to accept any idea that fills the void and offers a reason.

For example, a young child who has not yet differentiated from his parents demands an explanation for their divorce. Not yet able to understand distinct personhood, and unwilling to assign failure to either of his parents, he personalizes the blame and concludes that it must be something he has done. He is willing to accept the fault is his and assumes the trauma is due to his inability to perform in some way. In our adult mind, with mature perspective, we can see the fallacy in that conclusion, but it becomes part of the child's paradigm. He accepts as fact that he is a failure because he has been, and is, unable to fulfill the duty of keeping his parents together.

What we believe to be true becomes our reality. It controls our thoughts, emotions and actions. When we believe lies, our thoughts, feelings and behaviors are sinful. When we believe the truth, it changes the way we feel and act.

Our worldview is subject to misinterpretation because we live in a sinful world subject to the continual bombardment of the devil's lies and distortions. Unless we regularly interrogate our beliefs, they may lead us astray.

For instance, a paradigm of rejection is based on the assumption that "I'm not lovable." This conviction then molds the rejected person's interpretations to confirm the original belief. In other words, every event will be rehearsed and interpreted as further proof of rejection. Each interaction is a test and the conclusion drawn is: "That proves that I'm still unlovable."

The quickest way to destroy arguments is to receive an explanation from God. When we interrogate a belief and ask Him for truth, His answer goes to our heart. It bypasses our mind, the normal processor of data. God's answer corrects our paradigm, formed from our conclusions to date.

However, God does not answer our every request. Consider Job, the righteous man who demanded answers from God. He had every right to ask God to explain the reason for his suffering. God chose not to answer his question. Instead, He asked Job a few of His own. I believe God turned the conversation to help Job discover how ill-equipped he was to handle all truth.

I know a man who lost a son in the war. He cried out to God in his grief and sorrow. In anguish, he demanded an explanation: "Why did You let my son die?"

God answered him with a question. "For you to understand, I will have to tell you why each and every son or daughter died in this war. Do you still want to know?" My friend wisely declined. He knew he could not bear that load of knowledge.

Because we are God's children, we have the right to ask Him for explanations. But God is not responsible to ensure our understanding of His reasons and responses. He is not searching for people who understand everything. He seeks relationship with people who will trust Him even when they do not understand.

We are created in God's image and designed to be in relationship with Him. The foundation of our relationship is faith, which is the assurance of things hoped for and the conviction of things not seen (Hebrews 11:1). Faith is not the opposite of reason, logic, or explanation; it is being assured of the truth of God without additional proof.

We destroy arguments with faith. Faith means we believe the truth. An argument, or our paradigm, is our current way of believing. Mind renewal changes our way of thinking, the result of our conclusions to date, and replaces it with the truth of God.

Tear Down Pretensions

In addition to destroying arguments, our weapons are able to tear down pretensions, also called lofty opinions (2 Corinthians 10:5). Pretensions are thoughts and ideas that are contrary to the knowledge of God. Truth cannot be recognized without the Holy Spirit, and in pretentious pride mankind raises himself to the position of highest authority. These "lofty opinions" occur when a man regards his thoughts as superior to the thoughts of God.

Our thoughts drive our emotions. Emotions are neither good nor bad; they are simply a response to what we believe to be true. For instance, we feel fear when we think we are in danger. We feel comfort when we think we are loved. We feel sorrow when we think we have lost something of value. It is not right or wrong to feel fear, comfort, or sorrow; each is appropriate in its time. When our emotion matches what God is feeling in any given situation we are in agreement with Him.

Let us consider six unpleasant emotions that are experienced throughout our life: fear, anger, sadness, disgust, shame, and hopelessness. We learn to return to joy from each of these emotions as we mature. If we fail to return to joy, these unpleasant emotions become chronic and influence what we believe and instigate pretensions. For instance, fear is a reasonable response to personal threat, but chronic fear makes us anxious and subject to panic. The pretentious thought is that God cannot provide or protect.

That is how the forces of darkness put us in opposition to God. Pretensions can flicker by quickly like a temptation. They can also linger and become the seed of a conviction, which is a strongly held opinion. The end result is that we are controlled by emotions that are not consistent with God's nature and hold convictions that raise themselves up against God's truth.

These pretensions are torn down by interrogating, or examining, their underlying emotions. For instance, anger is a primary emotion carried along by fear, a demand for justice, or a desire to control. When it is giving expression to a demand for justice, the lofty opinion may be: "I am the only one who can make things right." This conviction is in direct conflict to the word of God that assigns vengeance to Him, and Him alone (Romans 12:19).

We are not to be controlled by our emotions so it is important to tear down pretensions. It is not wrong to have opinions, thoughts or ideas, but it is "desperately wicked" to hold them in higher esteem than God (Jeremiah 17:9). We take the arrogant thought captive and make it obedient to Christ (2 Corinthians 10:5) by interrogating what we believe and allowing God to replace our false conclusions with the truth. This is mind renewal (Romans 12:2).

Weapons for Healing

The weapons we fight with are not the weapons of the world. On the contrary, they have divine power to demolish strongholds. We demolish arguments and every pretension that sets itself up against the knowledge of God, and we take captive every thought to make it obedient to Christ. - 2 Corinthians 10:4-5 (NIV)

This language of weaponry focuses on destroying strongholds, demolishing arguments, and tearing down pretensions. The objective of the devil is to steal, kill and destroy, but these weapons are used to reconcile, redeem and recreate. This is what turns our weapons into "weapons for healing!"

The Spirit of the Lord is upon Me, because He has anointed Me to proclaim good news to the poor. He has sent Me to proclaim liberty to the captives and recovering of sight to the blind, to set at liberty those who are oppressed, to proclaim the year of the Lord's favor (Luke 4:18-19).

Jesus introduced His ministry with these words and then He went about forgiving, healing, casting out demons, and raising people from the dead. At times He spoke a word of truth that set captives free, at other times He rebuked an unclean spirit to overcome oppression, and always He shared the good news of the Kingdom.

Ask Him to guide your prayers of intercession. He will speak to you by the Holy Spirit through memories or visions, feelings or sensations, a word or Scripture, or perhaps an insight.

"Truly, truly, I say to you, whoever believes in Me will also do the works that I do; and greater works than these will he do, because I am going to the Father. Whatever you ask in My name, this I will do, that the Father may be glorified in the Son. - John 14:12-14

PART II:

SPECIFIC

PRAYER STRATEGIES

Chapter Six:
Money

For the weapons of our warfare are not of the flesh but have divine power to destroy strongholds. - 2 Corinthians 10:4

We demolish strongholds with spiritual weapons of warfare. We do not wrestle against flesh and blood, but against the rulers, against the authorities, against the cosmic powers over this present darkness, against the spiritual forces of evil in the heavenly places (Ephesians 6:12).

Though there can be many strongholds, we have observed three major areas where the effects of the spiritual forces of evil can be expected: money, sex, and power. We will address each in turn, using examples to show the patterns of a stronghold and prayer strategies that overcome them.

And my God will supply every need of yours according to His riches in glory in Christ Jesus. - Philippians 4:19

How is it possible that money could become a stronghold when we have Bible verses like this one? God is our Provider, and He has unlimited resources at His disposal. The Psalmist expressed this truth by writing: "He provides food for those who fear Him; He remembers His covenant forever (Psalm 111:5)." As long as we put our faith in Him we are immune to the schemes of the enemy in this matter.

However, our sinful nature causes us to take on responsibility for which we have no authority. We strive and worry because we know that it is beyond our own ability to provide for our needs. Jesus commanded that we not be "anxious about our life, what we will eat or what we will drink, nor about our body, what we will put on. Life is more than food, and the body more than clothing, and our Heavenly Father knows we need these things (Matthew 6:25-26)." Our anxiousness is sin that opens the way for the enemy to establish a stronghold.

Learn from Me

The Fortress

The stronghold of money uses fear and greed to control or manipulate resources. The philosophy of this authority can be summed up as "give and take." It is a mindset that is built upon the premise that resources are limited. Fear is fueled by the belief that I might not get what I need or that I might lose what I have acquired. Greed is fueled by a similar belief: that I might not get enough unless I take or keep it for myself.

When we tear down this stronghold we are able to replace it with God's Kingdom economy. His Kingdom economy is based upon love and generosity and can be summed up as "give and receive." The Kingdom economy is built on the understanding that there are unlimited resources, which in turn allows us to fulfill the command to be fruitful and multiply. Love takes the place of fear, and generosity takes the place of greed. We are able to demonstrate love by sacrificing from what we have, knowing that God is the Provider, and He will always provide more than enough.

The stronghold of money introduces the lie that we must provide for ourselves and deceives people about the character of God as Provider, and that He provides more than enough.

The Spirit of Mammon

Jesus taught about treasures in heaven that cannot be destroyed and compared it to treasures on earth that erode and are consumed. He then explained the principle of servitude: "No one can serve two masters, for either he will hate the one and love the other, or he will be devoted to the one and despise the other. You cannot serve God and [Mammon] (Matthew 6:24)."

Money is a medium of exchange. Its value is assigned and accepted by those who use it, or completely lost if they deem it worthless. Money does not exist outside of this use as a medium of exchange; it is not a person or being and has no intellect or will.

The spirit of Mammon, on the other hand, is a spiritual being. He is a ruler within a stronghold, having intellect and will. He interacts with intent to inflict his will on others. He is not the only spiritual being to exercise influence in this realm, there are others with specialized areas of authority, such as a spirit of greed, fear, pride, envy, and the like.[1]

We demolish the stronghold of money in the heart of the person by breaking down its walls, overthrowing the false authority, and expelling the rulers.

Prayer Strategy

The primary symptoms of a stronghold over money are worry, anxiety, greed, and idolatry. Any preoccupation with money is a signal that should be investigated. The prayer strategy interrogates the underlying belief about money so it can be replaced with God's truth. It usually includes spiritual warfare, such as expelling a spirit of Mammon, spirit of fear, spirit of greed, or spirit of pride. A step of forgiveness is often necessary: to receive forgiveness for lack of faith in God, or to extend forgiveness to those who oppressed the person financially. In some cases, a "deed of repentance" or step of faith is warranted, such as tithing, performing an act of generosity or destroying an icon of the stronghold.

Here are the prayer strategy steps:

1) *Ask God to reveal the root of this stronghold.*
2) *Confess the false belief and ask for truth.*
3) *Forgive offenses and break off generational curse.*
4) *Proclaim God as the Highest Authority and denounce the stronghold.*
5) *Identify the stronghold's ruler and accomplices.*
6) *Cast out the ruler and accomplices through a spiritual transaction of authority over spirits.*
7) *Confess the Lord as your Provider.*
8) *Accept a Kingdom economy lifestyle.*
9) *Check for "deeds of repentance."*

The healed person has renewed confidence in God as Provider, a generous spirit, and a true sense of contentment in all circumstances.

Poverty Mentality

A poverty mentality is a paradigm in which a person views himself as poor. It comes from flawed beliefs about resources, such as "there is never enough," "I don't deserve better," or "I must be satisfied with little." It is expressed in emotions such as fear, anxiety, insecurity, embarrassment, or hopelessness. It often leads to either a victim or entitlement mentality.

Poverty mentality can come from a cultural influence, where a people group has been financially oppressed, or from a generational influence where a family line has been poor. It can also be borne out of low expectations as a hedge against disappointment. In some religious cases, it finds a root in false piety or even as a means to demonstrate great faith.

— Learn from Me —

A poverty mentality believes there is never enough.

Carly was a single mom. She cared deeply for her boys and worked tirelessly to provide for them. She had divorced her husband, but not before his gambling addiction had put them deep into debt. After many years of diligent work, she had paid off the debt, purchased a house, and established a solid career with a good income.

Though Carly gave God the credit for her success, emotionally she was still in poverty. She filled her pantry to overflowing with staples and provisions. Still, on payday she went to the grocery store to stock up and soon excess groceries were tucked away in the garage. Though her family could have survived for months on the surplus in that pantry, she continued to accumulate. The spirit of Mammon had control of her emotions about food and she was anxious about having enough to eat. She was unable to trust God as her provider.

Carly recognized that she was trapped in an old way of thinking. She confessed to God her lack of trust in Him as provider and received His forgiveness. She chose to forgive her ex-husband for putting her in a financial crisis that led to her poverty mentality.

When I checked in to see how she was feeling, there was still a temptation toward fear. She had "what-if" thoughts about losing her job or being unable to work. There was a ruler of the stronghold at work behind the scenes. I cast out that spirit of fear and asked God to replace it with a fresh infilling of the Holy Spirit.

As Carly prayed in thanksgiving to God for her new freedom, He reminded her of the many times He had come through for her. She knew in her heart that He would never forsake her.

— Learn from Me —

A poverty mentality believes God provides the bare minimum.

Jerry and Diane spent many years as foreign missionaries before joining a parachurch organization closer to home. They had been in faith-based ministry since Bible college and appreciated how God provided for their needs.

They believed in the work they were doing but felt awkward about asking for support. They barely survived and always tried to get along on less, cutting corners wherever possible. When they received a large gift, it made them feel even more uncomfortable. Money became a source of conflict, pitting their faith against their comfort.

Jerry and Diane asked God to reveal the source of their money conflict and He showed them that they had a poor impression about missionaries. Their poverty mentality was rooted in the belief that missionaries, especially foreign missionaries, had to be poor. It had been signaled to them by their sending organization and modeled by other missionaries. They concluded that God would faithfully care for them by providing for their bare minimum needs.

I prayed aloud, bringing that thought to God on their behalf, and asked Him to reveal His truth in the matter.

"He owns the cattle on a thousand hills!" Diane blurted out. She was slightly embarrassed at how quickly and firmly the statement came out.

"And what does that mean to you?" I asked. "Why did God remind you of that verse just now?"

"It means that He has more than enough to take care of all of our needs, not just the bare minimum."

"Does that feel true to you?"

"Mostly. I mean, I know it to be true in my head. But I don't know if it really feels all the way true," she confessed.

We found the verse in the Bible and she read: "Not for your sacrifices do I rebuke you; your burnt offerings are continually before Me. I will not accept a bull from your house or goats from your folds. For every beast of the forest is mine, the cattle on a thousand hills (Psalm 50:8-10)."

"We've been trying to sacrifice for God," Jerry explained. "We should sacrifice to Him instead. He doesn't need us to save Him money."

They each confessed that they were limiting God's right to bless them, which is false piety. Their countenances changed as they received forgiveness, and suddenly there was peace in the place where conflict had been.

"Now it feels true!" said Diane with a smile. "He really does have more than enough, and it is fine with me whatever He wants to provide. It is all a blessing."

A stronghold was demolished that day. The authorities were forced to surrender to the highest Authority. Jerry and Diane surrendered their will which had been limiting God's blessings, and they began enjoying His extravagance.

— Learn from Me —

A poverty mentality believes "I deserve nothing." The root of this belief is often generational. For instance, some of the older generation grew up in or right after the Great Depression. They learned to be frugal and instilled those values on their children. Even though the environment has changed, the values continue to be passed along. There may also be cultural roots driving a poverty mentality. For example, those whose ancestors were an oppressed people group may still view themselves as slaves, servants, or laborers. They may live under false limits and lack the ability to perceive a Kingdom economy that provides more than enough.

In some situations, this belief is the result of a person's own conclusions. They may have committed a sin and assigned poverty as their penalty. They may believe in some sort of cosmic force or karma that has precluded them from receiving blessings. Healing prayer questions the belief that "I deserve nothing" and allows God to speak truth in its place. God is loving, kind and generous with those who know and love Him.

A poverty mentality operates from fear. Jim was a successful professional and a workaholic. He continued to drive himself to near exhaustion, although he had already accumulated a substantial net worth. He admitted that he was motivated by fear. He worried that he would not have enough and prided himself on preparing for every possible risk. He wanted a "fail-proof" financial plan to appease his fear but was too clever in inventing disastrous scenarios. His fear and pride trapped him in a vicious cycle. He needed to be healed from his poverty mentality.

A poverty mentality sometimes believes it is morally superior to be poor. This belief may be fueled by religious examples, such as a venerated saint who took a vow of poverty. It is an act of love to give to the poor, and it is fitting to honor Saint Teresa of Calcutta, for example, for her demonstration of love. It is also fitting to appreciate Job, Abraham, David and Solomon who cared for the poor while being materially blessed by the God of unlimited resources.

Similarly, God commands us to manage our world wisely and provide stewardship over all of creation. Managing one's carbon footprint, conserving natural resources, and maintaining a healthy environment are aspects of this responsibility. However, the current ecology movement often uses guilt and the mindset of limited resources which lead people to a poverty mentality.

Orphan Mentality

The person with an orphan mentality believes he must provide for himself. This belief undermines faith in God as Provider. Some respond with extreme self-reliance and engage in unhealthy striving or become workaholics. Others respond with a victim mentality and become dependent upon charitable organizations. Still others respond to the conflict by becoming devious or manipulative for personal gain. The orphan mentality is often accompanied by an inability to bond, which leads to a self-centered perspective. The primary symptoms are fear, anxiety, and insecurity about money and food.

An orphan is a child that has lost both parents before he is able to care for himself. Orphans are produced in warfare, plague, and poverty due to shortened life spans of parents. However, an orphan mentality can also be the result of a lack of parenting for any reason, such as death, divorce, or deployment.

The prayer strategy for orphan mentality is to interrogate the belief that I must provide for myself and allow God to present Himself as Provider. It may also include spiritual warfare to expel the spirit of Mammon and other evil spirits. This stronghold will likely have expressions in other areas besides provision, because the self-reliance and inability to bond affect the spiritual and emotional realms as well. For instance, an inability to establish healthy relationships with other people translates into a weak relationship with God.

The result of healing is a renewed mind and confidence in God as Provider, which leads to a generous spirit and a renewed ability to relate with others.

— Learn from Me —

The orphan mentality believes "I have to provide for myself."

Pete got his first job working after school and saved his money diligently. He bought his first car within months of getting his driver's license. He paid for his own clothes and put himself through college by doubling up on classes and working the night shift. He was proud of the fact that he was never a burden to anyone and gave God credit for giving him good health and a strong work ethic.

Pete came for prayer because of stress-related health issues. He was unable to ease back on his responsibilities, even though the doctor had warned him about the side effects of too much work. He wondered if he could be cured of being a workaholic or if it was how he was wired. Maybe he needed to pray for a stronger constitution to go along with his industrious identity.

We asked the Spirit for guidance and Pete was surprised to learn that he had an orphan mentality. Although he had spent his first two years in an orphanage, he really thought it made no difference to him since he could not remember that far back. His adoptive parents had always loved him and treated him like one of the family, but the belief that he had to provide for himself rang true.

Before we went to prayer about this issue, Pete wanted to know if it was wrong to work hard. He had always been diligent and everyone had appreciated this aspect of his character. I assured him that God appreciates our greatest effort when our will is aligned with His, but when we are operating in our own strength it creates conflict. He agreed that the stress he felt was a sign of conflict in this area of his life.

Pete confessed the sin of placing himself in God's role as Provider and asked for forgiveness. I acted as witness to the spiritual transaction and watched as his body relaxed. Then we took authority over the spirit of Mammon who had been driving him to exhaustion. We took turns commanding him to leave.

Learn from Me

Pete continues to be well respected in the business community and among his friends because of his hard work, but he has a new mindset about God as Provider. His work is now a sacrifice of praise, and he is thankful for provision from the hand of God rather than his own efforts.

— Learn from Me —

The orphan mentality affects latchkey kids. Although they are not orphans by the traditional definition, they are often left to their own devices. They learn at an early age to make do for themselves, and this attitude tends to follow them.

Tom explained that he had a house key when he was in first grade. He kept it tied around his neck with a string. After school he would watch Scooby-Doo and wait for his mom to get home from work. They would have a late supper before bedtime. She switched to the night shift when he was ten, but that was worse. She worked from eleven to seven but was either asleep or getting ready for work most of the time Tom was home. He learned to get his own supper.

The idea that God was his Provider was a complete surprise to Tom. He had come to believe that God helps those who help themselves, and he was used to making do. He was not sure he needed anyone, even God, to help him out now that he was able to fend for himself.

"God, Tom believes he must fend for himself and that his provision is from his own hand. Would you reveal to him what he needs to know about You?" I prayed.

"Oh, my goodness!" he exclaimed. "I remember boiling hotdogs for my dinner. I must have been six or seven, because I had to reach over my head to take them off the stove. The only reason I didn't boil my face off is because God was helping me."

Tom discovered God's love for him through that mental image and it changed his attitude about provision and bonding. He forgave his parents and gave glory to God for His faithfulness. He thanked God for being his unseen companion and protector.

— Learn from Me —

The orphan mentality can become a victim identity. When a person feels unable to provide for himself, and has not accepted God as his Provider, he may become dependent on any source of income available. He may treat debt as provision until that well dries up, and then he may consider welfare or disability income as provision.

Marion was orphaned and adopted into an abusive family where she lived until she was ten. She was rescued from there but placed in one bad foster situation after another for the next eight years, until she outgrew the system. She came to believe that she was unlovable and a burden to others. In her later years she qualified for government assistance and was able to live independently through aid programs and rent subsidies.

Marion's monthly assistance checks were insufficient, so she got into the habit of advancing herself cash through a payday loan company. The extremely high fees and interest rates kept her indebted to them and she became discouraged. She asked for prayer.

The spirit of Mammon had latched onto Marion and held her in bondage by the debt and orphan mentality. She was quick to confess her reliance on government programs and repented to God as her Provider, accepting by faith that He could help her dig out of that horrible trap.

Marion felt challenged by her daily life, but she chose to walk in faith. She applied some gifts to her debt and operated in strict stewardship over everything God provided. It was a struggle, but over the next year she learned that her faith in God was well founded. Ultimately, she paid off everything she owed and began to experience increased health as well.

Slavery Mentality

Do you not know that if you present yourselves to anyone as obedient slaves, you are slaves of the one whom you obey, either of sin, which leads to death, or of obedience, which leads to righteousness? - Romans 6:16

Learn from Me

A slavery mentality is a paradigm in which a person calculates his worth based on his production or position. This economic view operates under the laws of obligation which characterize the worker as a drone rather than a being. The slavery model operates and exists in an exchange of effort for provision, protection, and other goods. The slave owner provides and protects for the sake of his investment and in exchange receives current and future performance from the slave.

Paul wrote: "you are slaves of the one whom you obey (Romans 6:16)." This refers to more than just money. If you become a slave to your career, employer, or boss then your identity will be determined by your training, title, or job description. If you become a slave to food, entertainment, or accolades then your identity will have to conform to them.

The biggest symptom of a slavery mentality is the inability to receive a gift. If your value is based on your production you will receive anything as if it is earned, and you will use it to evaluate your worth. If your value is based on your position then every gift is treated as an obligation, and it will be received as if to settle a debt or carry a burden. A slave has no opportunity to receive a gift as a demonstration of unconditional love. Every gift has a string attached.

The obvious solution for this condition is to cease responding in obedience to worldly things and connect your allegiance to God and His righteous ways. This sounds like serving God as a slave, but we have a better promise! The older brother in the parable of the Prodigal Son was a cautionary example of such slavery. God wants to treats us as sons and heirs!

> And because you are sons, God has sent the Spirit of His Son into our hearts, crying, "Abba! Father!" So you are no longer a slave, but a son, and if a son, then an heir through God. - Galatians 4:6-7

The prayer strategy to overcome slavery mentality is to confess and receive forgiveness for being a slave to worldly things. In the forgiven mindset you are able to receive the gift of sonship from God. It may be helpful to ask Him to confirm your status as son and heir. He may give a sensation of welcome and acceptance, a picture of belonging, or a scripture that confirms His promise.

— Learn from Me —

Kristen struggled with finding acceptance. She was a lovely young lady with a great deal of charm, but deep down she wondered if her life was just a show. She sought approval in her work and from her friends but felt she could not freely express herself without a great deal of concern about how she would be assessed. The lack of freedom was a symptom of slavery.

We asked the Holy Spirit for guidance to find the root of her issue.

"I remember how I felt on my birthday while I was growing up. My dad would always get me a gift, and usually a nice one. But I felt he gave it to me because he had to. It was his obligation as my dad to give me something. I didn't feel loved by it, but more like I was a responsibility for him as a daughter," she said.

"Does it feel true to you now that when you receive a gift it is more out of obligation than love?" I asked.

"Yes. I even feel that way toward God, when it comes right down to it. I know that God loves me, because He is love and He created me. But I don't think God really likes me. He has to love me, but He's probably not very happy about it."

As we explored her feelings and conclusions she recognized that the slavery mentality had been her guiding principle. She was a slave to the opinions of others and had never received unconditional love. She had tried to accept God as her provider but she assumed there were strings attached to everything He gave. She either had to earn it, or take responsibility for it, or pass it along to someone in greater need.

Kristen quickly agreed to ask God for forgiveness and prayed a sweet prayer to her Abba, Father. She was immediately filled with peace.

"Wow, that's a whole new way of thinking!" she exclaimed. "It's like a light switch just got turned on in my head, and I'm seeing things from a completely different perspective."

Her freedom has increased each day since that prayer time. She no longer works for money or affirmation but participates in her Father's business. She is free to enjoy gifts from God and others and has become generous in demonstrating unconditional love to her family and community. She has a new sense of purpose and joy in her tasks. Her mind has been renewed.

Hoarding

Compulsive hoarding is a physical response to emotional pain. Hoarders acquire and are unwilling to discard large quantities of objects, often to the point that their living area becomes crowded and potentially unsafe. They may be aware of their irrational behavior but unable to control it. They may be embarrassed by it and withdraw from others as a result.

People that have grown up in poverty may collect things of dubious value, often quoting the adage: "waste not, want not." Their environment can be described as cluttered or even chaotic. They see value where others see junk and may take pride in their ability to protect that value. They are collectors compelled by "bargains" and are reluctant to discard anything for less than its perceived value.

The prayer strategy for this condition is the same as for poverty mentality. We want the person to discover how he came to take on responsibility for his own provision and then ask God to renew his mind, so he can release that responsibility back to God. There may be a step of obedience as well, often an act of generosity toward others.

Hoarding disorder can also be associated with experiences of having possessions taken away by force, physical abuse during childhood, or forced sexual activity. Hoarders are frequently described as indecisive, procrastinators, resistant, and unmotivated. They may save worthless items, such as junk mail, old magazines or catalogs, and the like.

The prayer strategy for this root cause is to resolve the emotional trauma rather than the physical expression. We ask God to reveal the source of the issue and then work through the spiritual transactions of forgiving. Once the legal ground of the sin has been redeemed the person can release the behavior that the trauma has caused.

— Learn from Me —

Jeff's house and yard looked like a junkyard; it was an eclectic mess of castoffs and antiques. Five years ago, his well-intentioned friends performed an intervention. They sent him out of town and arranged to have all the junk carted off in his absence, but now it looked like the same old place. He wished to be free from this but lacked the self-control.

We asked the Holy Spirit for guidance and discovered quickly that he had always felt deprived as he grew up. He was jealous of the things other kids at school had, but his parents would not give in to his frequent requests. He tried to provide these extras for himself through any cunning means he could.

He confessed the sin of being his own provider and received forgiveness. I asked him to check into his heart to see if there was anything else standing in the way of his freedom.

"Well," he said. "I once sold a door for a '66 Mustang for over three hundred bucks. I got it for twenty-five. It's not wrong to make a nice little profit like that, is it?"

We talked a little more about that transaction and how often something similar had happened, which was infrequent. Then I asked him if he had a gambling addiction.

"Not anymore!" he said proudly. "What brought that up?"

I explained how a gambling hit keeps the dream of gain alive in the addict, and how a "junk-to-treasure" hit accomplished the same thing in him. He quickly agreed that he was not free from his gambling addiction, though he avoided casinos and lotteries. He received forgiveness for idolatry, which is worshipping the "hit" instead of God and felt a new sense of peace come inside.

Jeff had a new purpose, and over the next several months he gave away or threw away his hoard of potential treasures. He was truly free, and his home and yard now provide evidence.

Greed and Pride

The advertising industry takes advantage of people who do not know their true identities. Products are presented as status symbols and as a way to project an assumed identity of power, wealth, or admiration. However, new cars, clothes, or toys are not able to change one's image or offer a sense of happiness or success inside them. Like other addictions, buying status symbols creates an appetite of its own which cannot be sated.

Greed and pride are judgmental attitudes fed by the belief that one person is better or more deserving than another. It leads to selfish behavior toward material possessions. This attitude can come from cultural upbringing, often modeled by parents and grandparents. The worldview of wealth can stand in the way of compassion for others.

Greed and pride often result in inner conflict when a person looks up to a rich uncle, a wealthy neighbor, a movie star, or some other icon. He may want to emulate that role model by being as powerful, wealthy, or admired as they are projected to be. However, dissatisfaction and frustration occur with the realization that he does not have the means to live in that glamorous way.

The prayer strategy for greed and pride is to confess the sin of judgment or prejudice toward others and ask God to reveal the true identity which is not defined by possessions. Then gratitude can replace lust and compassion can replace selfishness.

Retail Therapy

Retail therapy is an addiction in which people try to buy comfort through their purchases. This behavior is fueled by the false belief that the purchase will recoup for a loss, or make one feel pretty, or fill some other empty place inside. The purchase brings temporary relief, but the addict is now driven to accumulate and may hide or disguise purchases to avoid detection.

In some cases, the purchaser buys the highest quality or best rated item, excusing it as an investment or valuable. In other cases, she may only buy at thrift stores or bargain centers, fueled on by the apparent savings. One of the key symptoms of advanced retail therapy is lifestyle irony. For example, a man might live in a hovel but drive a fancy car, or a woman may not have food or groceries but wears the latest fashion.

The prayer strategy is to discover the conflict in the person's life that he or she is trying to resolve. Ask God to reveal what she believes to be true that causes this conflict. Then that belief can be released as God provides truth in its place.

For example, Tina constantly bought cute things for her house, but it did not compensate for her dysfunctional family. Marcy bought clothes at a high-end store, convinced that she would return them later, but never did. Stan bought a new car each year because everyone in his small town remarked about it.

God showed Tina that she needed to invest in the relationships in her family to solve the dysfunction. He showed Marcy that her beauty came from within, not from what she wore. He told Stan that it was better to hear "good and faithful servant" from Him than to win the admiration of everyone in town.

Stealing

Let the thief no longer steal, but rather let him labor, doing honest work with his own hands, so that he may have something to share with anyone in need. - Ephesians 4:28

Learn from Me

The act of stealing, taking something that does not belong to you, is sin. The prayer strategy for removing the effects of this sin is to accept forgiveness as the Holy Spirit brings conviction and leads the sinner to confess and repent.

However, adopting the identity of a thief, one who steals, is a sinful condition because it takes on a false identity. The prayer strategy is to discover the person's identity in Christ as a replacement for the false identity.

It may be helpful to learn how the person took on the identity of a thief in the first place. In one case, the label was conferred on a boy by his mother who repeatedly called him a thief throughout his life. She escalated the act of sin into a false identity with her word curses. When I led him in a prayer to forgive his mother it opened the way for God to give him a new identity. We then asked God to break off the word curse, and immediately the man felt free from the stigma which he had formerly felt powerless to overcome.

> *Let the thief no longer steal, but rather let him labor, doing honest work with his own hands, so that he may have something to share with anyone in need. · Ephesians 4:28*

The Apostle Paul commands the thief to exchange his stealing ways for doing honest work with his hands. This exchanges an identity as thief for an identity of industriousness and generosity. In fact, this is one of my favorite examples of "deeds according to repentance" (Acts 26:20). The opposite of stealing is earning, and the opposite of being a thief, which is taking, is being generous, which is sharing. The repentant person has a new identity that helps care for those in need by allowing God to redeem his efforts to earn what is needed.

Chapter Seven:
Sex

Anyone who does not love does not know God, because God is love. – 1 John 4:8

Sex as a stronghold deceives people about the character of God regarding intimacy and love. It twists and perverts the way relationship is understood and expressed. For example, innocence with God is holiness and purity, but outside of Him it is naiveté. Intimacy with God is union, but outside of Him it is codependence. We must break down the stronghold of sex to restore sexuality as the gift God gave for uniting a man and wife into one flesh (Genesis 2:24).

The Fortress

The stronghold of sex operates under the authority of the world which uses lust and power to control or manipulate others for selfish reasons. The lie that feeds this stronghold is that love is self-focused, whereas God's love is self-sacrificing. As long as the object of love is self, all expressions of it are in direct conflict with the ways of God.

We tear down this stronghold by appealing to God's authority over sexuality and love. When we live according to His laws and commandments we will experience blessing. Those that choose to deny His ways will be subject to the consequences of their sexual sin.

The Spirit of *Porneo*

There are many demons and spirits that operate within the stronghold of sex, but the spirit of *porneo* seems to be a high ranking one. We use the Greek word here from which we get our word for pornography, and which literally means "fornication." This evil spirit takes control over people and leads them into sexual sin.

The gateway for these demons is sin committed by the person who breaks the commandments about sexuality. However, sometimes the open door was from a sin committed against the person by someone else, usually before the person was mature enough to make that choice on his own.

Prayer Strategy

The primary symptoms of a stronghold over sex are lust, adultery, perversion, dysfunction, and manipulation. Any preoccupation with sex can be investigated with prayer. The spirit of *porneo* and other unclean spirits oppose healing in this area and spiritual warfare is to be expected. A step of forgiveness clears the legal ground that has allowed this stronghold to reign in the person's life.

1) *Ask God to reveal the root of this stronghold.*
2) *Confess the belief and ask for truth.*
3) *Forgive offenses and break off generational curses.*
4) *Proclaim God as the Highest Authority and denounce the stronghold.*
5) *Identify the ruler and accomplices.*
6) *Evict the ruler and accomplices through a spiritual transaction of authority over spirits.*
7) *Accept God's definition of love and intimacy.*
8) *Repent to a lifestyle of purity.*

Sexual Abuse

Sexual abuse is an egregious sin because the victim suffers consequences even as an unwilling participant. At the very least it is a loss of rights, but it is also a loss of innocence. The victim of sexual abuse is open to attack by the dark forces of this stronghold and becomes subject to its authority. The primary symptom of sexual abuse is a lack of freedom to express love and engage in intimate relationship with others.

Sexual abuse often goes unreported, especially when the abuser is a family member or known to the family. The victim may be led to believe he or she had a role to play and is complicit in the abuse. The victim may believe that reporting it will not make any difference to them or the abuser. Often the victim suffers from lack of voice because of the perceived danger of telling what happened.

The prayer strategy for sexual abuse is to ask God to reveal the root of the pain. There may be reluctance on the part of the victim to engage in this step for fear of re-experiencing the original trauma. However, when God invites someone to return to a place of pain, He is faithful to guide them through it so they can receive perfect comfort in its place.

The next step is to take an account of the sin and forgive the abuser of the offenses. Be a patient witness to this spiritual transaction rather than risk missing some aspects of what the offenses have cost. Generational curses are to be expected, and it is appropriate to break them off with an additional spiritual transaction. The release of these offenses is paramount to complete healing.

Children that are sexually abused have lost their innocence, which God gives to guide us through the growing up process. For that reason, they may have distorted boundaries, if any at all, regarding sexuality. However, at some point in their maturing process they have made the choice to practice these sins. They must confess and be forgiven to find true freedom.

When the forgiveness has been completed, ask God to restore purity to their heart and mind. This will allow them to gain a new understanding of God's good gift, and He will be able to redeem sexuality for His intended purposes.

Lust and Pornography

Lust and pornography are listed together because each are examples of self-absorbed sex. God created the good gift of sex to help man and wife become one flesh. When it is not shared for this purpose it only serves for self-gratification. It is limited to the world's way of "give and take" rather than operating according to God's principle of give and receive.

Lust is a craving for something that is not mine to have or is not good for me. When a craving is for something good we call it a desire, like an intimate union with my spouse. However, when my purpose for sex is self-gratification, conquest, greed or pride it is sin. Selfish sex is lust, even in a marriage, and it may also manifest as infidelity.

The prayer strategy for freedom from lust begins with the confession of self-importance. Then ask God to reveal the root issue that is prompting the lust. It may be rejection, lack of nurture, desire for comfort, or other needs. Confess those needs and invite God to fill them in His way.

Pornography is an expression of lust and a gateway for the stronghold of sex. This sin dehumanizes people and attempts to disconnect the emotional and spiritual realms from sex. It uses images and icons to dissociate the body from the person until it is perceived as nothing but an object. It uses fantasy to deny the spiritual connection and manipulate the emotions in a self-managed and self-pleasing way. It is a lie based on an illusion that destroys innocence and perverts intimacy.

The prayer strategy for pornography begins with forgiving whoever is responsible for its introduction. This probably occurred between the ages of eleven to thirteen for men, but sometimes as early as seven or eight. One of the offenses that needs to be forgiven is that innocence was destroyed by these images. This sets his future wife up for failure because he has established an impossible physical standard in his mind, to which no real human can measure up. He has conditioned himself to compare one person with another, and the seed of dissatisfaction has been planted.

The prayer strategy for dealing with pornography use by women also relates to rejection and loneliness. She must forgive the one who introduced her to pornography and receive forgiveness for accepting it as a counterfeit for relationship. The emotional attraction of this sin is built in fantasy, and a feeling of control drives the addiction.

Pornography takes advantage of a young person's natural curiosity and uses it to implant lies that dehumanize and desensitize. It presents a physical solution to stress, loneliness, boredom, rejection and other emotions that distract the mind but does not solve the problem. It is habit forming and becomes an addiction, but the short-term effect wears off quickly and exposure must be steadily increased for any effect to be felt. Soft-core pornography destroys innocence and hard-core pornography perverts the idea of intimacy. Ask God to reveal the pain or need that the addiction is attempting to fill.

The next step in the prayer strategy is for the person to confess as sin his choice to engage in pornography and lust. When that has been forgiven, he can ask God to fill the need or comfort the pain that he had been self-managing.

It is likely that sexual sin has opened the door to generational curses which must be broken off. Also, since this is a stronghold, the intercessor can anticipate evil spirits. Take authority over them and cast them out so the person is set free from their tyranny. Ask God to renew his mind so purity will replace the innocence that was lost, and to restore a godly understanding of intimate relationships.

— Learn from Me —

Roy was just eight years old when he found the magazines in his father's dresser drawer. At first, he thought it was weird but he was intrigued and snuck back in from time to time to take another look. One day his mother caught him in the act and scolded him in front of the rest of the family. He felt ashamed and dirty. He came to believe that sex was dirty and that there was something wrong with him. He assumed he was obsessed with sex.

When Roy came for prayer, he had been addicted to pornography for about twenty years. It had destroyed his first marriage and was undermining his second. He had tried to quit but was unable to break the habit for more than a few months. It seemed something would happen to reignite it, such as a fight with his wife, a business trip out of town, or bad news about a project at work.

131

We had asked God to reveal the root cause of his addiction and that was when he recalled discovering the magazines when he was eight. He quickly agreed to forgive his father for allowing him to be in harm's way. He forgave his mother for shaming him, and he received forgiveness for engaging in pornography. We identified a spirit of *porneo* and cast it out, and then talked about how to hold the territory if that spirit ever attempted to regain entry.

Roy reported back to me that he went directly home and spent several hours deleting files on his computer and destroying images he had saved "just in case." Then he shared that God must have given him new eyes, because he saw his wife in a whole new way!

Casual Sex

The sexual union of man and wife has been euphemistically called "making love," but the stronghold of sex has completely demeaned the value of God's good gift. In our society, sex is typically treated as a personal right, devoid of emotional or spiritual commitment. The "free love" and personal expression that began in the 1960s has confused the following generations who have learned to treat sex with contempt and confusion.

When sex is treated casually it is robbed of meaning. It is seen as an expected or possible outcome of an encounter, a physical response to arousal, or a moment of mutual self-gratification. In this context, the union of two souls is an unanticipated side-effect of the activity, to which many are completely oblivious.

It is appropriate to ask God for mind renewal regarding sex. Many marriage and other relationship problems are affected by the misuse of this powerful tool for unity. The prayer strategy is to repent to purity, break off soul ties, and ask God for guidance toward holiness.

— Learn from Me —

Eric and Emily wanted a stronger relationship, but little grievances kept cropping up between them. They had been married for six years but had been together for ten. I met privately with Eric and asked how they had first gotten together. He shared that they had met at a party while in their early twenties. They both partied a lot during that stage of life, and they really hit it off. Each had been sexually active and indiscriminate, but with no sense of shame or guilt. It was how they were raised and seemed to be the way everyone partied. They had agreed to leave that in the past when they got married.

Eric was shocked when I described to him the purpose and power of God's good gift. He had never heard about the union of two souls before and was intrigued. Then his interest turned to sorrow.

"I didn't know. I lost my innocence and purity before I knew it was something to preserve. I wish I had it all to do over again, but I can't change a thing," he lamented.

I led him through a prayer of repentance and he felt the power of God's forgiveness take the place of his sadness. He renounced the rules and authority of the stronghold and agreed to follow God's commands. Then I acted as witness as he broke off soul ties with each former partner, as God called them to mind. He smiled through his tears as the freedom began to take effect.

"Wow, I can imagine living in purity with Emily now! This is a completely different way to think, isn't it? Did you know God could reset this?" he asked in amazement.

I smiled and confirmed. God has power over the stronghold of sex, and when His authority is followed there is no longer any room for control or abuse from the enemy. This was the beginning of a new way of relating for Eric and Emily.

Promiscuity

I adjure you, O daughters of Jerusalem, that you not stir up or awaken love until it pleases. – Song of Solomon 8:4

Promiscuous behavior is a product of our culture. Sexual intimacy is not regarded as a great gift to share, but as a tool for personal gain. This mindset changes when a person accepts a Kingdom culture rather than living in the ways of the world. If promiscuity persists in the Christian it is likely due to a sexual addiction or past trauma.

Whereas casual sex is devoid of meaning, promiscuity assigns the wrong meaning. Sex becomes a tool for control, affection, provision, or any other need. It is completely divorced from its true intention of bringing a husband and wife into oneness.

Innocence protects a young person from having to deal with "the knowledge of good and evil." When that innocence has been stolen, the child is left without proper boundaries for interacting with others. King Solomon warned against premature arousal or awakening of sexual desire for this reason.

A paradigm, or worldview, is formed by conclusions made during one's life experiences. A promiscuous person may have come to assume that sexuality is a primary characteristic of attractiveness, or that physical contact is a demonstration of affection, or that sexual intimacy is the only way to express love to others. These false beliefs affect how they present themselves and how they respond to others.

— Learn from Me —

Alexa was filled with the excitement of a new believer, having accepted the Lord as her Savior just weeks before. She knew her life had changed, and she was putting on the new self. She needed help. Her persona was flamboyant, but her heart was filled with fear of vulnerability. Her wardrobe was provocative, but she disliked the attention she got. She wanted authentic relationships but she feared rejection and struggled with shame.

We began our prayer time with praise and thanksgiving for what God had saved her from, and for the wonderful future He had in mind for her. When I asked if she was ready to tear down the stronghold of sex in her life she quickly agreed.

"You have been forgiven, and you are a new creation in God's sight," I explained. "He sees you as holy and righteous, and your past has been redeemed. He invites you to accept that redemption for each part of your past, both the sins you've committed and those committed against you."

"Where do I start?" she asked.

"We ask God," I answered, and then led her in a prayer of discovery. God took her to several representative memories, each of which introduced an offense or offender that needed to be forgiven. God is gracious, He does not make us go through each event. He can forgive an offense in one event and apply that forgiveness to every related offense. Alexa was relieved to discover this truth.

After we had worked through redeeming Alexa's past, I asked God to reveal what she could know about her true identity and future.

"God sees me as a little girl that loves to twirl! I can see myself dancing in His presence, without any shame."

Alexa was renewed in her mind through these visions and the truth God showed her. She replaced her wardrobe over the next several weeks, finding new outfits that helped her be true to her real identity. She is still expressive, but not with the flamboyant flair that demands attention. Her creativity is quickly obvious, but it reflects the character of God rather than the stronghold of sex. She was excited to share with me about the transformation. It had been easy for her and each new choice she made seemed to fit her better and better.

Perversion

Perversion and sexual immorality are defined as the pursuit of unnatural desires, according to Jude 1:7. The literal Greek translation for "unnatural desire" is "strange flesh," meaning a deviation from what is normal or proper. As stated earlier, sex is God's good gift to unite a husband and wife as one flesh. Anything else is unnatural and immoral. When a person acts in a way that conflicts with God's design it causes pain. The pain from this stronghold is spiritual, emotional and physical.

Sometimes people are perplexed that they have pain, because they believe they have done nothing wrong. However, they take their cues from a culture that recharacterizes all manner of perversion as normal and natural. The pain is real because truth is not based on public opinion or social mores. Perversion is borne out of trauma, and all expressions of immorality and unnatural desires lead to pain.

Perversion disrupts healthy relationship. It opposes God's ways and interrupts a person's ability to communicate with Him. It opposes God's plan and warps relationships between one person and another. These broken relationships create pain in the spiritual and emotional realms.

There are many symptoms of emotional pain, such as fear, sorrow, rejection, anger, and hopelessness. Perversion becomes addictive because the behavior it evokes does not fill the void that prompts it. In other words, the rejected man cannot win enough sexual conquests to fill the void created by his rejection. The affirmation, appreciation, or admiration he is seeking from someone can never be filled by a substitute.

— Learn from Me —

Ryan asked for prayer because he wanted a better relationship with his wife, but all his efforts toward that had not been successful. He knew something was standing in the way but did not know how to resolve it. We began by asking God to reveal whatever stood in the way of Ryan and his wife having a one-flesh relationship.

"The thing that quickly came to my mind was sexual abuse," he stated. Then continued, "I was abused by an 'uncle' when I was six or seven. I don't know why this should come up, because I've already dealt with it. But that's what came to my mind as you prayed."

He assured me that he had forgiven the man who had abused him, as well as his parents for not protecting him. I helped him check back into the memory to see if there was any residual pain, but there was peace throughout.

"Have you struggled with same-sex attraction?" I asked.

"Why do you ask that?" he wondered in amazement.

"It's a pretty consistent pattern I've observed with men that have been sexually abused, especially those who were abused at a very young age," I answered.

"I didn't know that!" he said. "I thought it was just me. I have struggled with it all my life, as far back as I can remember. I thought it would go away when I got married, but it hasn't. I talked with my wife about it many years ago, but she didn't know how to respond. It's not been a subject I dared bring up again. I don't talk about it with other men, either."

"Would you like to be healed?" I asked.

"More than anything!" he quickly responded.

I led him in a spiritual transaction to reaffirm that he had forgiven his abuser and those that should have protected him. Then he confessed to God that the attraction was something outside of his control and asked for forgiveness. We took authority over a spirit of perversion and commanded it to leave in the name of Jesus. Then we prayed thanksgiving together.

Ryan reintroduced himself to me at a prayer workshop about two years later. He beamed as he reported about the health of his marriage. Then he shared that he has been completely free from same-sex attraction ever since we prayed about it. He thanked me for praying with him and admitted that at the time he did not think he could be healed from it. Now he is living proof that God sets the prisoner free!

Chapter Eight:
Control

For although they knew God, they did not honor Him as God or give thanks to Him, but they became futile in their thinking, and their foolish hearts were darkened. ·
Romans 1:21

The stronghold of power is all about control. God is Creator and holds the ultimate authority, but He will not abuse anyone by forcing His will on them. Nevertheless, man in his fallen nature is compelled to raise himself above God, just as the devil was. As Paul writes in the first chapter of Romans: "Even though they knew God, and who He is, they did not honor or respect Him as God (my paraphrase)." Paul goes on to describe the descent into lawlessness that happens because their foolish hearts are darkened. The description of that depraved life is filled with abuses of every kind.

The Fortress

What lurks protected inside this fortress of control is vile and hurtful, but rather easily identified. The list, as detailed in Romans 1:21-32, includes lust for impurity, idolatry, unrighteousness, malice, envy, foolishness, faithlessness, heartlessness, and ruthlessness. Everything from perversion to murder is used to control and dominate. The need for dominance may come from an over-inflated ego, a condition in which the power monger believes he or she is the only one capable of exercising authority. It can also come from insecurity, where exercising power or authority is a vain attempt at self-protection.

We tear down this stronghold by confessing the sin of pride that leads to self-exaltation and recognize God in the position of highest authority. As long as we are in rebellion against God, this stronghold will drive us to dominate others. Once we have surrendered to Him we will be able to relate with others in love rather than competition.

The Spirit of Rebellion

When our daughter was three and a half, she put her little hands on her hips and said: "You're not the boss of me!" This is a typical response for a child that age who is learning to differentiate identities and discover the nuances of freedom, responsibility, and choice. Of course, we gently explained to her that we were, in fact, the boss of her. This was not up for negotiation but assigned to us by God. He is the Boss, dad and mom are under His authority, and our daughter is under our authority while growing up. We transferred authority to her as she was able to handle it, and she became "the boss of me" at maturity. Now, God is still the Boss, and she is directly under His authority.

When the issue of authority is not worked out properly, a child takes on responsibility for which she has no authority. This gap in the chain of command should not exist, but it becomes a lace in which a spirit of rebellion grows. The person with this spirit resists authority, sometimes passively and sometimes aggressively. Their attitude is that no one can tell them what to do, and they do not have to follow rules.

Our western culture celebrates independence, and this is fertile ground for the spirit of rebellion. The tendency toward strong self-reliance can be expressed as an unwillingness to submit to authority, including the laws of the land. The person becomes a law unto himself, and he rejects or resists any rule that displeases him. Two symptoms of this condition are holding oneself above the law or redefining the law to suit one's purposes.

Prayer Strategy

The symptoms of the stronghold of power are stubbornness, self-righteousness, and taking control of others. As stated earlier, any time one person overrides the free will of another it is abuse. It is called physical abuse when he uses physical means to control someone. It is called emotional abuse when he uses emotions or feelings to control. It is called spiritual abuse when he uses spirituality to force compliance.

We demolish the stronghold of power by submitting to God as Supreme authority and removing any form of rebellion that rises against Him. The abuse of power may come from cultural influence, generational curse, personal choice, or a combination of these factors. We take an account in prayer to extend and receive forgiveness. Finally, we repent to living under God's rules and ways as our authority.

— Learn from Me —

We have noticed that a rebellious spirit is often behind addiction. I first discovered this in a prayer appointment with Mike, a long-term smoker. He was willing to let God heal him, because he had failed repeatedly trying to quit on his own. We asked God to reveal the source of this addiction.

"I started smoking when I was fourteen," Mike said.

"Lord, show him why he started smoking," I prayed.

Mike laughed and said: "My dad told me not to. When I was fourteen, I'd do anything my dad told me not to!"

When I asked him if he had a spirit of rebellion back then he quickly assured me that he still did. I led him in a prayer of authority over the spirit of rebellion, commanded it to leave, and invited God to replace it with a contrite heart. After thirty years of addiction, he became a nonsmoker that day!

We have used this prayer strategy effectively against many forms of addiction since that time. The spirit of rebellion may have been invited in many years before, but it will not leave on its own accord. It is often most evident by the power of addiction, but it shows up in other ways as well. Being rid of this unclean spirit allows people to come under God's authority in other parts of their life as well.

Authority Issues

The chain of command begins with God. Jesus said that all authority in heaven and on earth had been given to Him (Matthew 28:18), and it was given by God the Father (Philippians 2:9-11). Authority is transmitted through a chain of command. The one who follows an order has all the necessary authority to complete it, up to the authority of the one who issued it. Anyone who operates outside of the chain of command is operating beyond his authority.

This is the basis under which we, as Christians, are able to take authority over demons and unclean spirits. We are issued an order to be disciples of Jesus, and we are commanded to do the things that He did. He commanded demons to leave, and we have the authority to do the same. As long as we are working under orders received from Jesus, we are fully able to destroy the works of the devil, because that was His purpose.

The reason the Son of God appeared was to destroy the works of the devil. - 1 John 3:8b

However, the chain of command is often broken in this sinful world. God's authority will not pass through someone who is not under His authority, nor can an order issued outside of His will be sourced by His authority.

One of the great biblical examples of this is found in the nineteenth chapter of Acts. In verse eleven it says that God was doing extraordinary miracles by the hands of Paul. Diseases and evil spirits came out of people by God's authority because of Paul's obedience. The seven sons of Sceva, a chief priest, attempted to exorcise evil spirits as well, but were not under orders by God or Paul. They were going outside of the chain of command, and it was quickly obvious that they did not have authority over the evil spirits (Acts 19:11-16).

Authority and control are powerful tools, but there are some personality types who are prone to abuse of control. Those gifted in leadership, administration, and as directors may be susceptible to such abuse. As we have seen in Chapter Four, the redeemed side of these traits help a community make forward progress. However, the unredeemed expression is controlling, self-serving, manipulative, and abusive.

Control is made up of power and direction, and people use different ways of relating to wield it in a relationship. They may use law, shame, need, or fear as the means to have control, but only love based relating is not abusive.[2]

A person with control issues most likely grew up without ever experiencing love based relating. They have learned from their family of origin or their culture how to protect themselves and their interests without loving one another.

The prayer strategy to overcome control issues will likely include forgiving parents and other authority figures who have modeled the abuse of power and control methods. It may also include the eradication of generational curses.

— Learn from Me —

Lorna, a pastor's wife, is no stranger to strife. Her husband is controlling and demands that she submit to him in all areas of life. He responds to any difference of opinion with Ephesians 5:22: "Wives, submit to your husbands as unto the Lord," which he uses as a goad for compliance.

"I love the Lord, and I love my husband," Lorna said. "It's just that sometimes I don't know how to walk in obedience."

I led her in a prayer in which she confessed her love as well as the conflict. Then we asked God to reveal His wisdom to help her resolve the conflict. I declared the promise of God that we know He hears us when we pray according to His will, and we have what we request (1 John 5:14-15). We agreed that God's will is for harmony in their relationship rather than conflict.

God gave Lorna a visual picture of His authority. She described a multi-layered fountain, with water flowing from one pool to another. I asked what she understood by that picture. She explained that the water represented authority, and that there was only one source.

"God is the source of all authority," she said. "When my husband is under His authority there is no conflict, but when he operates in his own authority he is trying to create another stream. I must follow God's authority wherever there is a difference between the two wills. But, I don't know how to honor my husband when he follows his own way."

I told her that she needed to ask God how to honor her husband rather than let him define the terms. God can show us a loving way to relate that overcomes conflict.

A few months later, Lorna gave me an update on her situation. She described a miraculous change in her husband that happened shortly after we had prayed together. God used her loving attitude to soften the environment around him. Her respect allowed him to consider his position rather than defend it, and God began to show him the places where he was striking out on his own. His heart was changed and they have come under God's authority together.

Retaliation

When a person is in danger the sympathetic nervous system's fight or flight response is appropriate. For those who are more inclined to fight, the response may persist beyond the triggering event, or even be triggered by similar but different events. This is often the case in the life of a person who has been hurt in the past and continues to take responsibility for meting out justice.

For example, a woman who has been abused may not have been able to fight off her attacker when it happened, but she takes vengeance against others. She believes that: "If I do not hold them responsible, then no one will and they will get away with their crimes." While it may be true that someone appears to get away with it, she does not have the strength or authority to hold others accountable for their sin. Only God can do that.

The retaliator is guilty of trying to control others in a vain attempt to reconcile the pain of the past through penalties and consequences heaped on the abuser. This is not an effective strategy, and only results in a root of bitterness. The retaliator may also take up an offense on behalf of others, often under the guise of compassion. However, it is not effective to carry an offense against someone for what they did to another. The most compassionate response is to forgive the offender.

The prayer strategy for resolving the retaliation response begins by identifying the primary or representative trauma at its root, and then choosing to forgive the offender. It may also be necessary to identify and forgive offenses committed against someone else that a person picks up on behalf of the one offended. Finally, it is necessary to confess and repent for taking on this form of judgment.

Narcissism

The narcissist controls others in an attempt to gain approval or acceptance. At the root of this disorder is a deep rejection and an inability to bond with others. As a result, narcissists use grandiose methods to deceive, devalue, debase, and show disdain for others in a vain attempt to feel better about themselves. They are extremely defensive against potential threats to their identity due to their fragility. They tend to be aggressive toward others because they lack healthy boundaries and relational skills.

A huge internal conflict drives narcissists into anti-social behavior. Their insecurity comes from not feeling loved and accepted, but their demands for respect and admiration drive everyone away. It is as if their only tool for relating with others is control and power, which opposes true relationship. When these means fail, as they always do, the narcissist resorts to greater and greater extremes. They attempt to hide their insecurity, even from themselves, and in the process alienate people around them. John Townsend does a great job of describing this dichotomy in his book, *Hiding from Love*. [3]

Narcissism and narcissistic personality disorder are challenging to work with because the subject typically refuses to see himself or herself as the problem. Their strategy is fully focused on blaming others for what is wrong. In our experience, the narcissist must hit bottom before he or she will abandon the control strategy. Unfortunately, narcissism generates so much drive and determination that the person appears successful in the eyes of the world. They can be wealthy, strong leaders, trend-setters, and fiercely independent. However, inside they are hiding deep pain.

The prayer strategy for overcoming narcissism must begin with compassion. The desperate actions of the rejected person will attempt to alienate the intercessor, but supernatural and unconditional love is the only antidote. Be aware of an orphan mentality or other rejection responses in the family of origin. Usually this trauma happened before age twelve. Listen in the prayer appointment for indications of poor parenting and parental abandonment.

The spirit of rebellion may have invited other demons to this situation, such as a spirit of anger or a critical spirit. The feeling of abandonment and an inability to bond create coping strategies that exploit others for personal gain. Watch for signs of a lying spirit as well, since one of the common symptoms is deception.

A narcissist has stunted emotional maturity which is revealed under pressure. They are likely to display symptoms such as tantrums, isolation, and paranoia. Treat him or her as an adult, but pray for them as a child, especially as God reveals the source of the pain. Only God is able to repay for the loss of bonding with parents and other meaningful members of the community, and only God can reveal and affirm his or her true identity in Christ.

Ask God to reveal truth into the narcissist's heart about how He sees him or her. God will fill the void with assurances of unconditional love and acceptance. Forgiveness is the only path to being worthy in God's sight, and He promises to grant that forgiveness.

Hyper-Responsibility

Good stewardship is a role assigned by God, and it includes taking responsibility for our actions and motives. However, when a person takes on responsibility that belongs to another it leads to hyper-responsibility. In fact, it is impossible to be responsible for something which is outside of your authority. Yet, some people are burdened beyond their capacity, and may give in to the stronghold of power in an attempt to control outcomes even beyond their scope.

Most hyper-responsible people are not out to hurt someone else with their power plays. More likely they are driven by good, albeit improper, intentions and they are surprised to consider the possibility that it is a form of abuse. They may be driven by pride, fear, or past trauma.

The pride-driven person has self-confidence, particularly in comparison to others. They are leaders, self-directed, and often strongly opinionated. They are the self-appointed go-to person in a crunch, and do not back down from responsibility. For instance, when the basketball game is in the balance and time is running out, this is the person that calls for the ball. They have the inner confidence that they are the best one for the job and are willing to live with the consequences no matter how it turns out.

Pride-driven hyper-responsibility is on a continuum. On the mild end are those with great personal expectations. They probably grew up in an affirming community and learned to believe in themselves. The prayer strategy with them is to point out that they may be treading on other's rights by their forceful nature. As they mature in their identity in Christ they will be more interested in the influence they have on others than the impression they make on them. They become disciple makers rather than controllers.

On the other end of the spectrum are those with great disdain for others. They probably grew up in a judgmental and critical environment and came to believe that no one else is able to take the lead. The prayer strategy is for them to overcome being judgmental and begin to see others as Christ sees them. It is good to walk them through a prayer of confession regarding their critical nature so they can have the compassion necessary to see people as they truly are.

Fear-driven people can also become hyper-responsible. These are the "mother hens" and fussbudgets that take control over hundreds of details, large and small, so nothing gets missed. For some reason they have learned to guard their heart with fear, and they may extend their realm to guard others with that same fear. They specialize in considering worst-case scenarios and have a strategy for every contingency. The problem of control is exacerbated when they make the same choices for others. Their overbearing care is stifling and draws others into fear rather than faith and hope.

The prayer strategy for fear-driven people with hyper-responsibility is to ask God to reveal the source of the belief that he or she is responsible. It may have come by assignment from a weak parent who wanted to be parented by their child. It may also come from their sense that chaos or disorder is inherently dangerous. Hyper-responsibility can be a learned behavior when the fear-driven person has taken responsibility to keep everyone safe from an abusive member of the family or community.

— Learn from Me —

I met with Bill for prayer because of the incredible stress he was under. He was in a hard-charging sales career that put "demand goals" on him to keep him motivated. His wife and kids required attention, and he had several half-siblings that constantly asked for help. He felt used up, and unable to make changes that might reduce the stress.

We asked God to reveal the source of this stress. Immediately a memory came to him.

Bill was five when his father left, but he was determined to protect his alcoholic mother. He decided to be grown up, able to care for himself, and to never be a burden to anyone. His mother noticed his efforts and bragged to her friends about how helpful he was, which really made him feel good. By the time he was in his early teens he could manage the household quite well, despite his mother's irresponsible behavior.

Bill finished high school and put himself through college while his mother had two more failed marriages and several boyfriends. Bill was the only stable one in a dysfunctional and fractured family dynamic. It was no surprise that everyone looked to him for advice, help, and an occasional gift or loan, but it was all one-sided. He was tired of it.

I led Bill in a prayer of confession for being hyper-responsible, and he felt a huge weight lift off him as he accepted forgiveness. He had been taking on more responsibility than he could manage ever since age five. God had made him a careful and intentional person, and his response to the initial need was to do something about it. His siblings had empathy and compassion but lacked the drive to try to make a change. Throughout the years, Bill accepted responsibility as it was handed to him because it was his natural response.

It was sin for Bill to make decisions for others, cover for their mistakes and shield them from consequences. He was acting against God's balance of authority and responsibility. We cannot take responsibility for things over which we have no authority. Bill took responsibility for his mother that belonged to her and God. When he understood this truth, he was quick to ask for forgiveness and felt a powerful release of all that weight he had been carrying. He was also free to extend forgiveness to his extended family for putting all that pressure on him.

When the stronghold of power was torn down, Bill was able to establish appropriate boundaries. He had to learn the difference between assigned responsibility versus assumed responsibility. He repented of assuming others' responsibility and his stress diminished immediately.

Chapter Nine:
Abandonment

Now faith is the assurance of things hoped for, the conviction of things not seen. - Hebrews 11:1

"We destroy arguments and every lofty opinion raised against the knowledge of God (2 Corinthians 10:5)." The word translated as "arguments" has its Greek roots in our word for logic. The King James Version translates it as "imaginations" and the New International Version as "reasonings." For our purposes, we consider arguments to be a person's paradigm, which is derived from their accumulated convictions based on their culture, experience, and other influences.

In the next three chapters, we will consider three major categories for these arguments, or paradigms: abandonment, rejection, and betrayal. When present, these paradigms have a significant impact on someone's identity. When a person is living in an identity that is different than their true identity there is conflict, and that conflict creates pain in the spiritual, emotional, and physical realms. When our fundamental idea of self is built on a lie, we must destroy that argument with mind renewal. God speaks to the heart and replaces the false belief with truth.

It is difficult, but not impossible, to discover these false conclusions on your own. The challenge is that what a person believes serves as their definition of normal. Most people do not have the capacity to question their worldview or paradigm; for most of us, what we believe to be true affects us with all the authority of truth.

We will begin by exploring the effects of abandonment. God had an interesting way to build community in the world. Every newborn is completely dependent on others for survival, and members of the community must provide and protect the infant for it to live and mature. Relationship happens where this need is met by the resources of others. The adult and child form a love bond as the giver fills what is needed. However, when the relationship is not healthy the child fails to thrive. Abandonment keeps a love bond from forming.

Abandonment can happen at birth when father and mother choose not to keep their baby, whether they leave it to die in the wilderness or transfer it to an orphanage or other institution. Adoptive parents may assume that their role has averted abandonment in their child, but our experience has shown that abandonment by the biological father and mother has an effect, particularly in the emotional realm, regardless of how well the child's needs were met by adoptive parents.

Abandonment can also happen during the formative years of childhood. The love bonds established at birth are supposed to grow and expand to meet every obstacle as the child matures. However, the ones who should provide that nurture may be missing in action due to death, divorce, deployment, or other reasons.

The effects of abandonment can also happen later in life. When a relationship is terminated, or an expected relationship does not materialize, a relational gap is left. Adults who are subjected to abandonment experience challenges in the same way children do. Their identity is attacked because humans are defined, in part, by how they fit into community. This cannot be resolved in a vacuum but must be discovered relationally.

Foundational Belief

Abandonment is one of the first attacks on a person's true identity. We are designed to grow up in community, and those that love us are the ones to affirm our true nature. When they see the wonderful gifts, strengths, and traits God has invested in us, they are to praise Him and proclaim them to us. That is the key way we discover our true self.

Abandonment takes away that important component, and we are left to guess who we are. Without those affirmations we may be tempted to guess who someone else thinks we should be, and then try to become that person. This path is fraught with risk and conflict, because unless someone truly loves me, they may send the wrong signals and I may chase a phantom identity rather than discover my true one.

People who experience abandonment early in life often have an inability to bond that affects all their relationships, and they become self-contained loners. They believe that they have to do everything for themselves and by themselves. Those that are abandoned later in life can have trouble bonding with others in similar roles or positions to the one that abandoned them. For instance, a woman may believe she could never trust enough to have another husband.

The loss of healthy bonding can also cause them to be desperate for affirmation. This can lead to codependency, which is clinging instead of bonding. They believe they were not worth staying for, so their true identity is not good enough. This leads to loneliness and a feeling of being displaced.

An orphan mentality is a common result of abandonment. The orphan believes he must protect and provide for himself. This may be accompanied with an inability to trust, either because they never learned how or because their trust was broken beyond repair.

Prayer Strategy

The presenting symptoms of abandonment issues are inability to bond, inability to trust, orphan mentality, and indications of codependency. The solution is for the person to bond with Christ, a bond that supersedes all others. There are two steps to the prayer strategy: forgive the abandonment and create a new bond with Christ.

Forgive the abandonment by addressing the following issues:

1) Who left?
2) What was their role?
3) Why did they go?
4) Forgive, accept their departure.
5) Who fills the gap?

The first question identifies who needs to be forgiven for the abandonment. The second helps take an account of what was missing because of their choice. The third step helps build compassion for the one who left. The fourth is the spiritual transaction of forgiving. Finally, the last step prepares the person to receive a new bond with God.

After I have led the person through these steps, I like to ask them if they are ready to receive the gift of God's presence to fill the void from the one who left. I assure them that God is able to fill it past, present and future. Then, when they have agreed, I lead them in a simple prayer of acceptance and allow God to demonstrate His presence to them.

Inability to Bond

An abandoned infant tends to have an inability to bond with anyone at all. However, a young person abandoned by a close friend may continue to bond with parents and others, but not be able to create new friendships with peers. A child abandoned by one or both parents through divorce is likely to have an inability to bond with other adults, especially authority figures. A spouse abandoned through death or divorce may have trouble bonding again at a deep, intimate level.

Special attention should be given to the person with presenting symptoms of abandonment to discover if bonding has been impaired. Pray for a healing in their willingness to trust again. When they choose to trust God, He will help them trust others to the extent that they accurately reflect His character.

— Learn from Me —

Rod had trust issues and struggled to develop and maintain relationships but he was surprised when God revealed that it was rooted in abandonment. He grew up in a Christian home and his parents had not divorced. He wondered how he could have experienced abandonment. We took it to prayer and asked God to reveal the root of his issues.

"My dad was always at work. He had to do a lot of overtime to help pay medical expenses, and when he was home he was too tired to engage with me. My mom had diabetes and depression and was on a lot of medication. It seemed like I mostly raised myself from the time I was in first grade. Although they were always in my life, I guess it really was a form of abandonment," he said.

As we dug a little deeper, he mentioned that his mom seemed to blame him for her medical problems because the diabetes came on while she was pregnant with him. He felt like his dad blamed him, too. He had been told not to be a bother to his mom, and he tried to obey.

After he forgave his parents, Rod felt a new sense of peace. He could imagine a new kind of relationship with his wife and kids that did not mirror the way he grew up. God healed his heart and set him up to love and be loved.

Isolation

The abandoned person may exhibit an inability to trust. If the abandonment happened early in life the ability to trust may have never been developed. If it happened later in life there may be a violent reaction to having trusted and then feeling betrayed. The latter example is more dramatic, but each needs supernatural intervention.

One of the presenting symptoms of abandonment is isolation, which is expressed as a tendency to withdraw, especially under pressure. This response can be observed in a wide range of people, from hermit to introvert. Some believe they are on their own, that life is insecure, and that problems tend to be their fault. Their coping strategy is to go it alone rather than take a chance on trusting someone else.

The prayer strategy includes a step of confirmation that the root issue is abandonment, then forgiving those who abandoned the person, and asking God to introduce safe people into their life with whom they can build relationships.

— Learn from Me —

Austin grew up in a chaotic home. He was the youngest of three energetic boys, although his brothers were ten and twelve years older than he. His father left them when he was six, his mother had a nervous breakdown, and his brothers promptly left home. He did not want to be a burden to his mom so he learned to care for himself. Video games and television were his easiest companions.

Austin asked for prayer because he could not break the pattern of anti-team behavior. He had been labeled as a loner at work and had trouble fitting in with a culture that valued teamwork.

He knew immediately that his tendency to isolate came from an inability to trust others. He believed he was on his own to handle problems, and no one would step in to help. By closing out others he headed off disappointment and forced himself to rely on himself. We prayed and asked God to renew his mind.

"I just saw a picture of God in my mind, and He was waiting for me to catch up to Him," he explained. "I felt like He was inviting me to walk with Him. I think that is what trust is supposed to feel like!"

I thanked God for showing him this image, and asked what else Austin needed to know to have a renewed mind.

Austin began to recall people from his past that had given him encouragement and comfort. At first, he described a person by role, such as a school teacher, and then he called them by name. He could see how each one had given him godly leadership and loving guidance.

"I get it now! God is showing me the people He used in the past to do His work. Since I can trust God, I can trust these people who are acting on His behalf."

We praised God for showing Austin the simple truth, that He is trustworthy and anyone He sends can be trusted, too.

Orphan Mentality

An orphan mentality can be a stronghold, as we saw in Chapter Six, but it can also be an argument or paradigm. A stronghold has its power in the spiritual realm, whereas an argument operates in the mind.

Abandonment is often at the root of this mind set which comes when a person believes he must protect and provide for himself. The key symptoms of this belief system are lack of trust and insecurity in relationships with others. The orphan does not think others will be willing to help and does not expect to be loved just for being themselves.

An orphan must be adopted in order to break the orphan mentality worldview. An adult with this paradigm must be adopted in the spiritual and emotional realms. Just as Jesus told Nicodemus that he must be born again (John 3:3-5), the orphan can be adopted. Practically speaking, the orphan needs to be involved in a community that offers relationship and presents them with opportunities to contribute.

In most cases we find that the person must confess his orphan mentality as sin and ask God to forgive. It may be helpful to discuss the truth that we are created as relational beings and designed to live in community. This is a picture of the church of the heart, which is the body of Christ (1 Corinthians 12:12).

As we have begun to adopt spiritual children, we have seen the need for reparenting and the importance of the role of elder. We need mature believers to help guide and encourage younger believers. God is able to renew the mind of the orphan, but they will need to add to their new mindset the relational values of a healthy community.

Hopelessness

Hopelessness is a mindset that believes circumstances cannot improve. It may be experienced as discouragement, sadness, chronic pessimism, or depression, and it can be the result of abandonment. The bonds of relationship give us perspective, encouragement, identity, and purpose. When we are missing these ingredients, it is hard to have faith for a favorable future.

Death is a form of abandonment, and though it may not be intentional, it still has a significant impact. The survivor may have lost her identity and purpose, as well as a source of encouragement.

A key step in the prayer strategy for this kind of hopelessness is to identify the loss and acknowledge it as abandonment. The grieving process has a purpose: to honor the past, accept the truth of the loss, and prepare for a new beginning. Hope returns when God is recognized as the source, and then the community can confirm His good will and purpose.

— Learn from Me —

Gerald had been treating his depression with medication for years, but he knew something was missing in his life. He came for prayer to ask God for help and direction. His father had died of heart disease about twelve years ago, his sister passed away within six months of his father, and then his mother died a year later. He lost his whole family in less than two years and never recovered. Now at forty-two he was trying to put his life back together.

I talked with him about the amount of loss and the purpose of the grieving process. Then we asked God to help guide us in our prayer time.

Gerald reported feelings of abandonment that arose from the time of loss and was nearly overcome by grief. I assured him that God answers our prayer by bringing us to the place that needs healing, and that he could trust God to complete the work.

"Are you willing to forgive your mother for abandoning you?" I asked.

"Forgive her?!?" he blurted. "How can I forgive her? It wasn't her fault. She didn't choose to die any more than my sister or father did."

"Blame has nothing to do with forgiveness. Blame is a tool for accusation and shame. Forgiveness simply recognizes a debt and chooses to release the one who left it. Although it seems like an unusual request to you, would you be willing to forgive your mother who left you, through no fault of her own, but caused a void in your life?"

Gerald accepted the invitation and forgave his mother. While he was at it, he forgave his father and sister too. He admitted that this was the first time he had heard that he could forgive an unintentional offense, and it made a big difference in his heart. The deep darkness lifted and clouds of confusion and sadness began to lighten. He smiled as the thought of a future dawned on him.

Hyper-Responsibility

Hyper-responsibility can be part of a paradigm that is formed in the trauma of abandonment. When a person in a role of responsibility leaves, it is likely that the one remaining picks up that responsibility. In some cases, the transfer is warranted but in other situations it is completely out of balance.

We have often observed the hyper-responsibility response in children that are abandoned, usually between the ages of six and twelve. This is the age when a person is learning their role in community and has very little experience or wisdom in how to assess appropriateness. Though they have only child-like maturity they take on adult-level cares.

We have also seen hyper-responsibility in surviving spouses who decide to step up to the plate and take on excessive responsibility in an attempt to honor their loved one. In other words, a widow may decide to run the family finances and affairs in the same way her husband did. If he was operating in his giftedness, and she has complementing gifts, she will find herself striving to maintain her husband's standards.

Every responsibility must be balanced by a corresponding authority, or the one carrying the responsibility cannot operate in integrity. For instance, you cannot take responsibility for how another person feels because you do not have the authority to control their feelings. Similarly, a child cannot take responsibility to run a household because he does not have the authority to do so.

The prayer strategy for this paradigm is to ask God to reveal the source of the responsibility and whether an appropriate level of authority has come with the assignment. If responsibility and authority are not in balance, the hyper-responsible one should forgive the one who gave them the responsibility and receive forgiveness for assuming it.

— *Learn from Me* —

Laura was eleven when her father died of cancer, just six weeks after it was detected. It was a crushing blow, and there were a lot of questions about how the family would survive financially as well as emotionally. During the memorial service, a well-intentioned aunt spoke to Laura.

"Don't cry, Laura," her aunt cautioned. "Your mom is going through a really hard time right now, and she needs you to be strong. Can you be strong for your mom and your little sister?"

Laura remembered fighting back tears and nodding her head. She wanted to be helpful, and there was no question about the pain. At that moment she took on responsibility for her younger sister and mother. The next twenty years were filled with conflict as she struggled with responsibility that far exceeded her authority.

I led her in a prayer to forgive her aunt for assigning her with this impossible task. Laura was visibly relieved to let it go. Then I asked her to release the responsibility back to God, to Whom it really belonged. She held her hand palm-up and prayed that God would receive back the responsibility. She gave out a spontaneous giggle, and then apologized. I explained that the feeling expressed by her giggle was evidence that she had returned the heavy burden to where it belonged. There was no need to apologize for doing business with God.

— Learn from Me —

Robert grew up in an unhealthy environment. Some of his earliest memories were filled with fear as he heard his father and mother fighting in the other room. He recalled that one or the other of them would be gone from the house for weeks at a time, but when they got back together it was the same old story. He spent quite a bit of time at his friend's house and was very conscientious because he felt safe there and did not want to do anything to jeopardize his welcome.

When Robert was in his early teens his dad left home for the last time. The rumor was that he had been put in prison, but it was not confirmed. His mother could not keep a job because of migraines and depression, so he supplemented where he could with part time jobs. By the time he graduated from high school he had a full-time job on a construction crew. His conscientious nature and willingness to work hard caught the eye of his manager and he never lacked for work.

He married and started a family, and he was a good father. He continued to provide for his mother and took on overtime to insure peace around the home. By all accounts he was successful, and everyone respected his strong work ethic.

Robert came for prayer because of some undiagnosed health issues. His pain would come and go, and the medical reports suggested an autoimmune disease may be the culprit. He had some fear that his ability to make money would be compromised, and he would let his family down. He took full advantage of the days he felt strong, and then tried to muscle through the days of pain.

As we prayed the Lord revealed that the pain was related to the stress he was under at work and home. I asked if he would be willing to incorporate Sabbath rest in his schedule and add healthy margins to his work. The way he looked at me proved that he did not have a clue about how to make that happen.

"Lord, Robert has confessed a great load of responsibility. Would You reveal to him how he came to have this responsibility?"

Robert explained that he first started taking on responsibility because it needed to be done, but then everyone around him allowed him to take on more. No one was there to warn him or even share the burden. It was his choice initially, but then it was just taken for granted. He had no idea how to get out of the middle of this.

I invited him to confess as sin the responsibility he took on for which he had no authority. Then I also led him in a prayer to forgive his family for taking advantage and heaping more on him. When he had done this, it brought a big smile to his face. He described the feeling as an internal vacation, and he had a sense of energy bubbling under that sense of rest.

"I'm not sure exactly what to say when someone gives me more responsibility, but I know God will give me the words," he said. "For the first time, I feel like I'm in charge of my life rather than it being in charge of me. This feels good."

I saw Robert again the following year and asked how he was doing. He smiled a great big smile and reported that God had saved him from the stress at just the right time. He had gotten a new job, had downsized their home, and felt like he could enjoy the blessings of God.

When the argument, or paradigm, of hyper-responsibility is destroyed the mind, will and emotions of the person are set free and he is able to follow the leading of the Lord. As long as the lie of responsibility has control over his mind, it is a never-ending role with an evil task master. Relinquishing the over-reach of responsibility, and letting God take care of the things that are His to care for, brings blessings and peace.

Chapter Ten:
Rejection

We destroy arguments and every lofty opinion raised against the knowledge of God, and take every thought captive to obey Christ. - 2 Corinthians 10:5

We destroy arguments, which are paradigms, by discovering what we believe to be true and making it obey Christ. Rejection has a huge impact on how a person perceives their identity. The conflict comes because we are created to be in relationship with others, and when we are rejected instead of loved it goes against God's design.

Rejection can happen at any age, and the earlier it occurs the deeper the paradigm shift tends to be. We believe rejection can be experienced in the womb, before a child is even born. This has come to our attention through prayer times, when God has revealed it to a person. We have also seen it manifested in our work and family. For instance, in our children's generation there are forty-three first cousins of which twenty-four are adopted, and of these, four were adopted at birth. Each of the adoptive families had both natural and adopted children. Yet, the symptoms of severe rejection are pronounced among the adopted, especially compared to the biological children.

Rejection is an attack against identity. The rejected one believes that "there must be something wrong with me, or I would not have been rejected." The depth of this belief corresponds to the nature of the relationship. In other words, when a mother or father rejects a child it is particularly hurtful. When a friend or peer rejects it may destroy part of the identity that is affected by that relationship, but there may be some compartmentalization that contains the damage.

Rejected people tend to strive for a new identity, one that will be acceptable to others. The class clown responds to peer rejection with an attempt to be funny, assuming that others will appreciate this character trait. The straight-A student may be responding to the belief that intelligence is the desired trait. As you can guess, rejection is often a driving force to cause someone to operate in a false character trait or the unredeemed expression of their strength.

We must replace any false idea of self, formed by the opinions of others, through mind renewal. We can ask God to speak to our heart and replace the lie with His truth.

Rejection can be overt, through words or actions, or expressed subtly with small and consistent cues. It may be done intentionally, but more often rejection is assumed by the one feeling rejected. It can be the result of divorce or shunning, but could just as likely be misunderstood cultural messages or expectations.

No matter how a person comes to the conclusion that they are rejected, the belief forms the basis of their paradigm and must be destroyed before their mind will be able to accept the truth of their identity.

Foundational Belief

At birth, we are completely vulnerable and utterly dependent on our caregivers. Not only do we need them for food, safety, and to manage our moods, but we also need their love and affirmation to discover our true identity. A mother's role is to nurture her child and demonstrate unconditional love. A father's role is to protect and provide for his child and affirm the emerging identity. If they fail in these assignments, the child's worldview is conflicted and he or she may try to find nurture, love, protection, and affirmation elsewhere.

I remember praying with David about his deep-seated rejection issues. The Lord reminded him of a time when his father was beating him and his mother did not protect. He was nine and came to believe that his mother did not love him enough to intervene.

"Mothers are supposed to love their kids, aren't they?" he asked through tears.

I agreed that this is the mother's role, and that she had made a grave mistake in not loving him. I asked him how his nine-year-old mind resolved the conflict.

"I thought there must be something wrong with me," he answered. "Something horribly wrong with me that neither my father or mother would love me. I believed I was unlovable."

These are very common conclusions drawn by a rejected person. Some similar forms that we have heard are:

1) *There's something fundamentally wrong with me.*
2) *I'll never measure up.*
3) *I have nothing to offer.*
4) *I'm not worthy of love.*
5) *I'm not_____ enough.*

On the last one, a person fills in the blank with whatever characteristic they have used to assess their failure. For instance, I'm not pretty enough, or smart enough, or thin enough, or big enough, or careful enough, or rich enough, and on and on it goes. The problem with this paradigm is that there is no standard by which the failure can be satisfied. He or she will always be what they believe themselves to be: a failure.

Prayer Strategy

The presenting symptoms of rejection on the aggressive side are codependency, people pleasing, manipulation, and control; on the passive side they are isolation, self-pity, sarcasm, neglect, self-loathing, addictive behavior, and an inability to forgive or receive forgiveness.

The first step is to interrogate the primary emotion or action demonstrated in the presenting symptom. Ask God to reveal the reason he or she acts or feels this way and listen for the root cause. Often a memory or idea comes to them that indicates the source of rejection. It may be extremely obvious to you, but irrelevant to them, so allow them to have the truth confirmed directly by the Spirit.

The next step is to invite the rejected one to forgive the one or ones who rejected them. Take a little extra time to help them take an account of the offenses and consider what the rejection has cost them. This step makes it easier for them to feel compassion which allows them to forgive more easily.

After forgiving, ask the Lord to reveal what the person believed to be true that fed the paradigm of rejection. A thought or conclusion they have drawn about their identity will come to their mind. Once they confess this belief you can take it to prayer and ask God to replace the false conclusion with His truth.

Use this grid to work through the process:

1) *What was withheld?*
2) *Who withheld it?*
3) *Why was it withheld?*
4) *Who must be forgiven?*
5) *What do you believe to be true about you?*
6) *Ask God how He sees you.*

Rejection comes down to a withholding of something. It may have been affection, affirmation, nurture, unconditional love, or similar things. Identifying what was withheld is part of the step of taking an account. But remember that rejected people may believe they do not deserve love and therefore may not understand what was withheld, or that being loved is a basic and valid need of every human being. The truth is that everyone deserves to experience unconditional love just because we are a creation of the Lord God.

Step two helps identify who must be forgiven, and step three sets the stage for gaining compassion as it often reveals a pattern of rejection formerly experienced by the one who has rejected us. Step four engages the spiritual transaction of forgiveness. Step five is a confession of the argument or paradigm that must be destroyed. Step six is the request to allow God to speak truth to replace the false belief.

Self-Loathing

Presenting symptoms of self-loathing cover a wide spectrum. When a person believes they are unlovable or that something is wrong with them, they may hate themselves as much as they perceive others hate them. This can find dramatic expression in suicidal thoughts, cutting, eating disorders, risky behavior, and drug abuse. Ironically, these dangerous actions may elicit sympathy from others, but pity is a poor substitute for love and acceptance, though the self-loathing person may prefer any attention over rejection.

Self-deprecating talk or humor is a subtler symptom of this condition. We call it a "first strike strategy" because it is an attempt at control, believing there is an advantage to be the first to speak the criticism or voice the complaint. Similarly, sarcasm, belittling talk, irony, and other forms of false humility are ways a rejected person may demonstrate their self-hatred.

Outlandish expression is a non-verbal symptom of rejection. Shocking style, dramatic tattoos, piercings, gender confusion, sloppy clothes, and aggressive behavior are attempts to force the main stream to reject. It is a cynical attempt at finding love, a vain hope that someone will accept them despite their counter-culture choices. The fact that these signals have become ubiquitous indicates that whole generations and cultures suffer from rejection.

— Learn from Me —

The life of a heroin user is filled with risk, and Jessica had been abusing drugs for well over a decade. Her parents divorced when she was young, and she and her brother lived with her dad. When he remarried she and her brother were moved into the garage, and their bedrooms were given to his new wife's children.

She was in and out of relationships with men by the time she was thirteen, and she acknowledged that she was looking for a father figure. The drugs, alcohol, and sexual relationships were not able to fill the void, and as her coping strategies grew, the danger increased as well. Somehow the risk of heroin overdose was not an entirely undesirable thought to her. At times she believed she would be better off dead.

She was pregnant with her third child when she came for prayer and wondered if there was any hope for her future or this child. She knew a little bit about God and was willing to give Him a chance to make the changes in her life that she was powerless to make.

Jessica described a time she and a friend tried to score a hit and were attacked and raped. The casual way she described the incident nearly broke my heart. Here was a woman, created in God's image, that had been subjected to such horrific treatment that this account was given like a news report about someone else. This dangerous lifestyle had deep roots.

God revealed the deep rejection issues as we began in prayer. It was her father that she needed to forgive first, and the memory that typified the rejection was when she and her brother were put out in the garage and only allowed in the house by invitation. It was difficult for Jessica to take a complete account because of the vastness and volume of offenses. However, when she released them in prayer, she felt a wave of peace fill her. She described it as the best feeling she had ever felt.

The Spirit continued to lead us in work of forgiveness for her mother, other family members that had abused her, and many that had mistreated her along the way. God is gracious, and there were several times when He called to Jessica's mind one representative person or event to forgive, and He used that as an example of a His willingness to forgive a long list of similar offenses.

Jessica found acceptance in a healing community and began to learn about her identity in Christ. The more she discovered about herself the more she fell in love with God. His unconditional love paid off the massive debt from being unloved which had accrued during her lifetime.

Façades

Rejected people might believe they do not measure up to proper standards and attempt to compensate by acting in a way they think will bring acceptance. This is especially true for those that believe "I'm not _____ enough." Whatever adjective they use to fill in the blank becomes their standard, and in most cases the standard does not match their true identity. For example, an expressive woman who was rejected by her parents assumed she was rejected for being too noisy. She believed she was not quiet enough. As a result, she presents a somber or pensive personality in an attempt to find acceptance.

People can be driven by wrong values and goals because of these misunderstandings. It is not that every trait to which they aspire is wrong in and of itself, but that it does not match their true identity. Classic examples of conflicted pairings we have seen include an impulsive temperament in a family that values order, or a mercy heart in a justice-minded home. The conflict comes when a person's true character trait is rejected and a foreign value is promoted in its place.

Other rejected personality types emulate traits they assume are desirable. For example, the stoic cowboy façade may be the personality depicted as preferred, and the rejected person learns to suppress emotions and guard his heart to depict it. Some symptoms mimic bi-polar disorder, as the experimenter swings between their natural self and the façade.

— Learn from Me —

"All my life I have been putting on disguises, trying to be the right man," Keith shared. "I was pretty quick to guess what someone valued, and then that is what I would present."

We spent some time in prayer, listening to God reveal Keith's true identity. At first Keith felt like he was trying to put on a façade for God, but then he realized that God was describing him from the inside out. He did not have to pretend because the truth was already there.

"I'm learning to let the 'fabricated man' die," Keith explained. "Now I can see the difference between the fabrication and the real me."

"Why don't you ask God to show you how to put the fabricated man to death?" I asked. "I would think that getting rid of this imposter would be much quicker by putting it to death than just waiting for it to die."

Keith quickly agreed and prayed for help. God gave him a clear picture of the mask he was putting on, and he saw himself shattering it with a hammer. Keith grinned as he shared the picture and how much he enjoyed smashing the imposter.

Fear of Man

Fear of man is a label we use for an unhealthy preoccupation with the opinions of others. The rejected person that operates in this paradigm tends to equate performance with acceptance. In their rejection they may have come to believe that they will never measure up, and that they have to find a way to appease others.

The presenting symptoms of this kind of rejection are stress, fear and anxiety. They are always looking for approval and may overcompensate with effort or change their behavior to maintain relationship. In most cases they assume the worst about themselves while inflating the standards they try to achieve. This creates an ever-increasing conflict that continues to fuel failure.

The prayer strategy for fear of man is to recognize that God's standards are perfect, and His assessment is sufficient. It is helpful to find the root of this fear, which may be an authority figure from early in their life. For instance, a strict father or teacher may have given the impression that their performance has been lacking, and acceptance is earned not granted. These conditions often come out of a performance-based or legalistic culture.

— Learn from Me —

Sofia was afraid to give the Lord control, but she admitted she was losing her grip. No matter how hard she tried, she could not handle all of her challenges, and the stress was causing emotional and physical problems.

"Lord, what is Sofia afraid of?" I prayed.

"I want to look good," she responded. "I'm afraid of letting people see me, especially right now. I always thought that I had to perform, to do all the right things."

"Lord, what is the basis of this need to perform?"

"Expectations from my parents immediately comes to mind," she answered. "Don't get me wrong, they were loving. We were a loving family, but you were expected to do the right things. I think I also put a lot of expectations on myself, assuming that if I didn't perform well I wouldn't be liked."

"Was this just your family's way, or was it part of your culture?" I asked, recognizing her Northern-European roots.

"Oh, it's definitely part of my heritage. Our family is very legalistic and responsible. I felt judged by my immediate family, but even more by my extended family and community. It always felt like, no matter how hard I tried, I just couldn't measure up. Someone would find fault with me, and I would feel bad."

We walked through forgiveness toward her family and culture for impressing performance-based relating on her. We prayed against the generational curse that had passed the legalistic and performance-based traits down the line. Then Sofia prayed to be forgiven for taking on responsibility that rightfully belongs to God.

"Lord, I have been running so long and so hard, running my own race, and not listening to You. Please forgive me, and can we get back on speaking terms?" she prayed honestly.

The Lord healed Sofia that afternoon. I asked her how she felt, and she was beaming. She said that she was excited to put this new way of thinking into practice, and she could see new ways of blessing others instead of feeling like she could never do or be enough to suit them.

I shared with her that she had been living under false pretenses by imagining the standards other people set for her. The good news is that God is the one who sets the standards. The bad news is that He is perfect and only accepts perfect obedience. More good news is that He has already forgiven her for each time she misses the mark: past, present, and future.

Overparenting

Overparenting occurs when a caregiver protects or provides beyond the needs of their child. Overprotection shields the growing individual from consequences, but also keeps them from important learning experiences. Overprovision creates a dependent or enabled child who does not learn to rely on God as Provider. Overparenting rejects the child's true identity while forcing him or her into an identity the caregiver chooses.

There can be many reasons for overparenting. In some cases, it is an extreme response to personal rejection. Ironically, a parent that experienced rejection tries so hard to be all and do all for her child that she inadvertently passes rejection along. In other cases, a parent lacks a personal identity and begins to over-identify in the role of mother or father. The problem with over-identifying in a role is that the role inevitably terminates, and the over-identification has no basis.

It is helpful to get guidance from the Spirit about the reasons for overparenting. When you pray with a child that has been overparented, he or she should be invited to forgive their parents. Then he or she can ask God to reveal their true identity, and they can begin to live up to that instead. They may need to communicate the change in their heart to their parent in order to reconcile the relationship.

When you pray with a parent who is convicted of this behavior, it should lead them to receiving forgiveness, first from God and then from their child, if the child is willing. The opposite of overparenting is not abandonment. Rather, it is a release of authority and responsibility in appropriate balance according to their maturity.

— Learn from Me —

Ramona was twenty-six and suffered from poor health. She had struggled with eating disorders in her teens and now had many food allergies. The doctors had not been able to fix a firm diagnosis on her symptoms, so she regularly went in for tests.

As we chatted, I noticed that she was tentative in her answers about how she felt or what she thought, as if she were insecure in her identity. I asked her about her home life.

"Oh, I have a very supportive home life. I'm an only child, and my dad and mom have always been there for me. I know they only want what's best for me, and I appreciate them for it."

"Are you living in the home you grew up in?" I asked.

"Yes," she answered. "I tried to get my own place a couple of times, but it didn't work out."

As she continued to describe her home life there was a hard edge to her voice, as if she were holding back emotions. She described her dad as controlling and her mom as comforting.

"How did that environment make you feel?" I asked.

"My dad made all my decisions for me and told me what to do, but the more controlling he became the more my mom came to my rescue. It seemed like she wouldn't let me make any decisions either. I still feel trapped. Like I can't move a muscle without permission."

"What do you believe about yourself that makes you feel trapped?" I asked.

"My dad thinks I'm too dumb to make decisions, so he does all my thinking for me. My mom thinks I'm weak and naïve, so she has to protect me. I don't know if it is true or not, because I've never been given the chance to try," she said through tears.

We began the process to forgive her parents, and Ramona began to take an account of the offenses. The first one that came to her mind was the idea that her dad and mom would not let her grow up. I explained that their control and comfort ended up stifling her emerging personality, which is a form of rejection.

"I never thought of that!" Ramona exclaimed. "I wondered why it felt like rejection when my dad and mom are doing the absolute opposite of rejection. But as you said that, it was like a light turning on."

She gladly forgave her parents for rejection, and immediately her heart was filled with compassion toward them. They had no intention of hurting her, but in their effort to do the right thing they overcompensated.

Over the next several months, Ramona's personality began to blossom. She grew in confidence and inner strength, and she began to share that confidence with her parents. They were able to release their grip and she was able to mature. There were still some rocky encounters through the transition, but Ramona had a better idea of who God created her to be, and she was following His plan.

Codependency

Codependency is a dysfunctional relationship where one person is defined by their role in helping another. The codependent one does not operate in his or her authentic identity, but rather in response to a perceived need. As long as the need / help dynamic is in place, both partners are trapped in this situation.

In most cases the codependent does not know his true identity, and therefore is destined to live into an identity defined by the needs of another. Then he can act in that identity as long as the role exists. When the role terminates, the codependent is likely to establish another enabling relationship to take its place. A vicious cycle occurs as this dysfunctional behavior disrupts the process by which he can discover his true identity.

Rejection exists anytime a true identity is denied, whether intentionally or otherwise. Codependency usurps a person's identity for its own purposes. Loyalty and responsibility are two of the most common reasons a person stays in a codependent relationship. The fact that it overrides their true personality is lost on them.

The prayer strategy for overcoming codependency begins with confessing and receiving forgiveness for taking inappropriate responsibility for the codependent partner. It is also important to distinguish between sympathy and compassion. Sympathy can be a form of judgment because it condemns a person to their current condition. Compassion is a tenderness in one's heart that can lead to forgiveness.

Finally, the codependent identity needs to be released and a new identity received to take its place. God is faithful to show a person who He created them to be, and they are in a position to accept this truth once they have released the old paradigm.

— Learn from Me —

Claudia has a big, tender heart and she hates to see anyone in pain. She is also quick to accept others as they are, because she has a past filled with mistakes and failures. She makes allowances for people in hope that they will extend the same courtesy to her and others.

She asked for prayer because she was feeling depressed and tired. Her husband, Jack, was fighting his addictions, but not making any progress. Each time he had some success her heart would leap, but then he would let her down again. It was about all she could take.

I asked God to bring us to a starting point for our prayer time, and Claudia realized that her life was being spent on Jack but there was no progress evident. She was afraid he would die of his addiction, and all of her efforts would have been in vain.

"Lord, I want to confess for Claudia that she has a great burden that she is trying to bear, and that she has fear. Would You please reveal the root of this to her?" I prayed.

Claudia looked a little startled after that prayer. She had gotten an image in her mind of a great burden being like a cloak around her shoulders, but it was beginning to choke her. When I asked what the cloak meant, she said it was responsibility.

"Lord, what would you like Claudia to do with this cloak of responsibility?" I asked.

"He wants me to take it off. He said it's not mine, and I don't have to wear it."

Claudia agreed to ask for forgiveness for taking responsibility for Jack, and felt the huge weight lifted as we prayed. Then I asked if she knew her true identity.

"Jack is my fourth husband," she explained. "Honestly, I think every time I've gotten married it was because I wanted to help someone. I keep falling for these guys that are a mess. And in every case, I wasn't able to help them overcome their problems. I guess I don't know who I am, outside of this pattern."

I asked God to reveal her true identity, and he gave her another picture. She described herself wearing a nice white uniform, the old-fashioned kind nurses used to wear. She thought it meant that she was designed to take care of people.

I opened my Bible and read these verses:

> *Blessed be the God and Father of our Lord Jesus Christ, the Father of mercies and God of all comfort, who comforts us in all our affliction, so that we may be able to comfort those who are in any affliction, with the comfort with which we ourselves are comforted by God. - 2 Corinthians 1:3-4*

"Claudia, God designed you to comfort those who are in affliction, but you need to comfort them with the same comfort with which you are comforted by God. You have been trying to comfort Jack and others in your own strength, rather than allowing God to comfort them through you."

Claudia had tears in her eyes as she considered this great gift of God. She acknowledged that her comfort had come from God and promised to comfort others in the same way. She was excited to live in her true identity. We agreed that the devil was sneaky. He had hijacked her true identity of comforting and turned it into codependency. Instead of being able to help people, she had been co-joined to their affliction. Mind renewal gave her a new bounce in her step and purpose for her life.

Chapter Eleven:
Betrayal

Betrayal destroys trust. It disappoints someone's hopes or expectations that are built on relationship. Betrayal leads to anger, bitterness, self-protection, independence, and cynicism. As a form of rejection, betrayal is an attack against a person's ability to belong and contribute.

The betrayer is stating, in essence: "I will sacrifice you for my benefit. I choose me first, no matter what it costs you."

Betrayal can be experienced in the workplace or on a team where relationships are developed around a common purpose or combined effort. Each member of the team has a role to play and the authority and responsibility to complete their part for the ultimate goal. If one member takes advantage of others it is betrayal. For instance, if one shirks his duties he betrays the others by forcing them to do more work. Similarly, if one takes credit for what another has done he betrays others who should receive the reward. The selfish choice of the betrayer destroys the hope of common purpose.

Betrayal often happens in families. A family is a team when the members have common bonds, shared history, goals, and dreams. However, if one family member makes a choice for his benefit no matter what it costs the others it destroys trust and relationship. For instance, a father experiencing a midlife crisis may opt out of his responsibilities, which betrays the family. Each family member is forced to compensate for his selfish choice.

The deeper the relationship, the greater the cost of betrayal.

> *For it is not an enemy who taunts me— then I could bear it; it is not an adversary who deals insolently with me— then I could hide from him. But it is you, a man, my equal, my companion, my familiar friend. - Psalm 55:12-13*

177

Betrayal in a marriage is an example of great cost. Two people promise to share hopes and expectations and a covenant binds them together to keep their dreams alive, but when these vows are betrayed the wounds are very deep. For example, adultery is a horrible breach of loyalty that destroys trust. Similarly, pornography, lying, hiding, and isolation are forms of betrayal. The betrayed partner experiences deep rejection because the offense denigrates the identity of each partner and their identity as a couple. In fact, rejection is a common byproduct of betrayal felt by everyone in the family.

We used to take sweet counsel together; within God's house we walked in the throng. - Psalm 55:14

Betrayal in ministry is particularly hard to overcome. It is unexpected for private agendas or selfish motives to invade a group of Christians who are commanded to love one another and operate as one body, yet we see it all too often. Betrayal can happen in churches, ministries, small groups, or in any team. When one or more of the members sacrifice the unity of the body for their personal needs or agenda, then all feel betrayed. The offense goes beyond the opposition of the common goal, it also harms God's reputation. The rejection can affect everyone in the community of believers, and trust is destroyed; trust between members and, in some cases, trust in God.

Trust is an expression of love, which is a reflection of the character of God, and betrayal breaks this trust. The betrayed does not want to be reconciled to the one who caused this pain. In fact, the thought of reconciliation may seem more repugnant than the constant pain of bitterness. They must be assured that God does not require, nor condone, our reconciliation with sin nature. We can only be reconciled to the righteous reflection of God in another. Forgiveness and reconciliation are two separate transactions. A person can forgive the sin of betrayal and not be reconciled to the sinner.

Foundational Belief

Betrayal is not fair. The offense precipitates a paradigm of unfairness and a worldview that trusts nothing. This cynical belief system undermines faith, hope and love. In its most severe forms it even believes God cannot be trusted.

A ministry betrayal may result in false conclusions such as these:

- I am disqualified from accomplishing my purpose.
- I have been operating in my calling, but it is now revoked due to this failure in ministry.
- My calling, or purpose, must not be of God or I would not have experienced this trial.
- My ministerial role has been terminated, therefore my calling is over.

These foundational beliefs are rooted in the trauma of betrayal but are not founded in truth. They create an argument, or logic grid, that is cynical of trust and leads to bitterness. The mind that holds these conclusions must be renewed by receiving the truth from God and operating according to His principles.

Prayer Strategy

The presenting symptoms of betrayal are disappointment, distrust, bitterness, and pain. Rejection is felt from the loss of purpose, or calling, and the marginalization of strengths and gifts. Remember that emotions are neither good nor bad, but a response to what we believe to be true. Allow the person to express sadness and disappointment in response to the betrayal, and then guide them in prayer to discover the root of the pain.

You can use this guide in your prayer process:

1) *What have you lost?*
2) *Who hurt you?*
3) *Why did they act that way?*
4) *Forgive the person (including echoes of the pain).*
5) *What has God promised you?*
6) *Who are you, now?*

Learn from Me

The first step in this prayer process is the same as the first step in forgiving: take an account of the offenses. Ask the person what they have lost to help them build a list of debts or offenses which they may choose to forgive.

Steps two and three are used to focus on the ones responsible for the betrayal. Identify all who caused damage and then find compassion in your heart toward them by asking what drove them to such behavior. If the betrayal is fresh you may need to ask the Lord to supply a seed of compassion. These two steps prepare the betrayed person to forgive.

The fourth step is a spiritual transaction of forgiving. Invite the betrayed person to confess and release each offense identified by the earlier steps. Advise them that echoes of the original betrayal may come to their attention in the future, and that this does not mean the forgiveness failed. Each echo is a new aspect or facet of the original offense which can be added to the spiritual transaction of forgiveness retroactively.

The next step is to ask what God has promised them. He may have already given them a promise that will be recalled to their mind, or you may need to ask God to reveal His promise to them now that the forgiveness has been granted. In most cases, God will reveal that He has a place, mission or calling for them, and that He provides an opportunity to serve.

Consider this opportunity to repair a broken relationship between this person and God. Ask God to reveal His response to the act of betrayal. The betrayed person may be assuming that God let the offense happen either because He was absent or distracted. Ask God to share how He felt about it, and that revelation will repair the broken relationship. In my experience, God gently shared that His heart was broken by the betrayal and it made Him sad.

Finally, include the question of identity in the prayer time. Guide the person to ask for truth and God will renew or reaffirm their identity in Christ. Confirm what the Lord reveals, and then ask the person what that means to them. They may already know what new beginning God has in mind for them, or they may need to accept by faith that He has a new assignment that will match their gifts and strengths.

Cast your burden on the LORD, and He will sustain you; He will never permit the righteous to be moved. - Psalm 55:22

King David detailed in Psalm 55 the betrayal he experienced from a friend, and Jesus used the same scripture to describe the betrayal He experienced by Judas. Anyone who has experienced betrayal can benefit by reading this Psalm because it articulates the offense and emotional response to be expected. Toward the end of the passage we read the important solution to betrayal: cast your burden on the LORD, and He will sustain you. This is a promise to claim.

Inability to Trust

The primary presenting symptom of betrayal is an inability to trust. There is an old adage: "Fool me once, shame on you. Fool me twice, shame on me." This saying acknowledges that breaking trust is shameful, but then adds that the greater shame is to trust again. Trust is a precious commodity and people despise its misuse. They would rather not trust than risk a second helping of betrayal.

Trust cannot be earned; it must be granted. For example, an unfaithful husband cannot earn his wife's trust. As long as she believes he is untrustworthy he will never be able to dispel her conviction. No matter how many years he goes without cheating on her, or how many temptations he avoids, or how many times he says he is sorry, the only way trust can be restored is if she chooses to grant it to him. Granting trust is an act of will, a choice that is made, not a conditioned response.

The one whose trust has been broken must first forgive the offense before she will be able to grant trust again. She may wish it had never happened or try to ignore the sin in hopes that the consequences will go away, but neither response will produce reconciliation. She cannot ignore her paradigm and pretend to trust again, but if she forgives she will be able to see her husband as a new creation to whom she can grant trust.

— Learn from Me —

Suzanne discovered that her husband had been cheating on her from before they were married. When they were engaged, she wondered if he was addicted to pornography, but she did not confront him about it. Years later he confessed. He had been living a lie and had not been faithful to her. His sex addiction had gotten worse over the years and he acted out with pornography, one-night stands, and prostitutes. He asked for forgiveness, and desperately wanted a second chance.

She was torn. On the one hand she believed sexual immorality was a reason for divorce (Matthew 5:32), but she also believed she had to forgive (Matthew 6:15). She wondered if she could forgive and what the ramifications would be.

"I feel like such a fool," she said in our prayer appointment. "I suspected something, but when I asked he made me think I was losing my mind. He's fooled me once and I'd be a fool to let him do it again."

"You've loved him, Suzanne," I answered. "It is not foolish to love someone; it is an incredible gift. When you love someone, you are not the fool. The one who refuses to be loved is a fool."

Her heart opened to consider forgiving him. It was still a tough decision because she had been lied to for over twenty years while the betrayal was happening right under her nose. Finally, she agreed that he could not change the past, nor prove his loyalty.

Suzanne was set free when she forgave her husband for infidelity, betrayal, deception and rejection. Her spirit rose, as if from the dead, and she had hope for a joyful future again. She could not imagine that it would include her husband, but she believed God had good things in mind for her.

This story has a happy ending. Suzanne's act of grace paved the way for her husband to receive healing, too. He was touched by her unconditional gift of kindness and he asked God for forgiveness. God forgave him and healed him from his addiction. The pattern of betrayal and rejection had been in his family for several generations, but God stopped it right there. They were reconciled with each other because they were each reconciled to God.

Loss of Purpose

*For the gifts and the calling of God are irrevocable. –
Romans 11:29*

Betrayal is an attack against identity. The Apostle Paul knew that the calling of God on his life was to preach the gospel, and he was compelled to bring the good news because it was his purpose, it was his true identity. He faced opposition in his ministry by his own people, the Jews. They betrayed him by stirring up dissension everywhere he went in an effort to thwart his purpose.

Betrayal in ministry is especially hurtful because we are called to unity in the faith, with Christ as the head. The common purpose of a ministry team should be established by God and maintained by the members. However, conflict arises when a betrayer begins to operate according to his own agenda at the expense of unity. As a result, decisions are made or actions taken that betray the common purpose.

If a person assumes his calling is defined by his role or job description he will suffer a loss of identity when that role is terminated. Instead, he must realize that his role is merely an expression of his calling, and that his God-given purpose survives betrayal.

For example, Paul had a calling, an assignment from God, to preach the gospel to the Gentiles. His first role was as a Jewish rabbi, or teacher, but he was excommunicated from the synagogue. His next role was as an apostle of Jesus Christ, but this title was challenged by the believers in Corinth and many others. Fortunately, Paul understood that his calling came from God, not man. His role could be destroyed, his position terminated, or his reputation marred, but he was under assignment from the Lord. His gifts and calling were irrevocable (Romans 11:29).

— Learn from Me —

Ryan loved his job as Family Life Pastor at his church. He had worked diligently to reconcile a couple of factions and enjoyed seeing greater community and fellowship in the congregation. He was a peacemaker, and it showed. Five years later he was out of a job and wondering what God might have in store for his family.

"Last year, at the annual meeting, an announcement was made that our church was chronically over budget and changes would have to be made," he shared. "The executive pastor said that budget cuts would mean some jobs would be lost. For the next several months everyone held their breath, and we prayed for more money to come in. This year the senior pastor and executive pastor each got a raise and I got a pink slip. I wasn't the only one to get fired, either. There were about six of us, but most of the others were part-time jobs."

Ryan felt betrayed by the church. He had lost his job, his church family, and his self-respect. As the leadership team informed the congregation about the cuts, they let people believe that Ryan was being let go because of performance as well as the financial constraints. He was not given opportunity to respond to those messages.

I led him through the steps of forgiving the leadership, the congregation, and the influential members of the church that failed to support him. Then I asked what he believed to be true about himself because of this betrayal.

"I'm not allowed to operate in my gifting, to pursue my calling," he answered. "They took that away from me, too!"

We went to prayer over this belief and I asked God to renew Ryan's mind. The Lord reminded him that he was created to be a peacemaker. He felt a burning in his chest, just like the first time God revealed this calling. He remembered several specific times he brought peace to others, long before he was hired as a Family Life Pastor.

"Lord, now I know the purpose you have for me," he prayed. "Please forgive me for doubting Your good gift in me. Forgive me for confusing my calling with my job. Forgive me for not trusting You to provide opportunities to obey Your assignment. I know that You are in control, and I accept whatever You have for me."

Ryan worked in construction for the next year and had many opportunities to be a peacemaker. He explained that his faith in God as provider improved and he was filled with anticipation for the next opportunity. He realized that his gifts and the calling of God are irrevocable.

Root of Bitterness

A root of bitterness comes from rehearsing and reviewing the pain or loss from an offense that has not been forgiven. As long as the debt is outstanding, the injured party is reminded of what he is due, yet doing without. The chronic sorrow over loss is an unresolved conflict which causes pain in the spiritual, emotional, and physical realms.

Betrayal is an injustice that causes deep pain. The steps of grieving are appropriate because hope and expectations have died. When the loss is not recognized and acknowledged, the pain continues unabated. It is illogical, but the one betrayed believes he cannot get over the injustice of the offense. As long as he believes that, he truly cannot get over the pain. However, if he is willing to acknowledge the loss and release the debt, the pain can stop.

In one case of severe betrayal, a woman declared that she just wanted to have nothing to do with her betrayer. She wanted to be completely free from any connection. When asked, she admitted that she had not forgiven, and in fact could not forgive because the betrayal was so great. I explained that there would be a connection between her and her betrayer as long as she was owed a debt. She is related to him as a bill collector as long as there is any offense outstanding. The only way to completely cut off all ties would be for her to forgive him.

The solution to a root of bitterness is forgiveness. No other remedies are possible because the offender does not have the means to repay or set the record straight. As soon as the offense is forgiven the root dries up and is blown away by the wind.

Vengeance

Beloved, never avenge yourselves, but leave it to the wrath of God, for it is written, "Vengeance is Mine, I will repay, says the Lord." – Romans 12:19

Vengeance, the desire for retribution, can also be a presenting symptom of betrayal. The desire for justice drives this attitude, whether someone has personally been betrayed or if they have picked up an offense for someone else. The Lord says that justice is His domain and He will take responsibility for it, but some injured parties want to usurp His authority in this matter. A person is overstepping his bounds in the area of responsibility anytime he acts as an avenger.

A justice mentality drives a person to try to exact payment or punishment for the offense of betrayal. This paradigm holds that a balance between good and evil exists, and the pain incurred by the injured party must be meted out in equal portion to the offender. Of course, this does not work because pain inflicted does not offset pain experienced, it just doubles the overall pain.

Another paradigm of vengeance is the self-assigned need to set the record straight or expose the sin. The one betrayed may be trying to protect others from trusting the one who has broken trust. They may hope to reveal the true, and evil, nature of the betrayer so others may be on guard and keep themselves from harm's way. In a way, it is an attempt to redeem the pain by using it as a warning for others.

— Learn from Me —

Tina thought the dark days were behind her. It had been five years since Craig told her he was having an affair. She was shocked and devastated. Their twenty years of marriage had never been great, but Tina was determined to preserve the family. She got counseling, worked on her challenges, and tried to forgive, but she was in a great deal of pain. The doctor diagnosed Multiple Sclerosis, and she doubted that she could fight this health battle, too.

She was diligent in working through her pain and saw some improvement with the guidance of the counselor, new tools, and renewed effort. Her health began to improve as well, and her doctor declared her Multiple Sclerosis in remission. Their son and daughter graduated from high school, and it seemed like there was hope.

The crisis reemerged six months ago. Craig filed for divorce. He explained that he was in love with the other woman and wanted to marry her. Despite his promises to the contrary, he had not stopped seeing her and now that the kids were out of the house he felt his obligation to this marriage was over.

Tina's heart was broken again. She struggled with depression and her Multiple Sclerosis came roaring back. It was her worst nightmare. Her doctor was shocked by the quick return and wondered if she had really been in remission. He said she would probably be confined to a wheelchair within a year.

When Tina came for prayer she could not sort through her emotions. The double dose of betrayal was unbearable and she wanted Craig to suffer. Her friends and acquaintances pitied her, but she wanted them to know it was all his fault. She wrote a scathing letter to the other woman, cursing her and castigating Craig. She felt like such a fool.

"Craig betrayed you as a wife, partner, and mother. You can't change him or force him to be an honest man. Are you willing to release him?" I asked.

"If you're going to ask me to forgive him, you need to know that I can't," she replied. "I don't want to release him. I don't want him to hurt others the way he hurt me. Honestly, I just want him to be dead."

"You are carrying that death in your body," I answered. "What he has done is evil, and there is no way to justify it. The wages of sin is death. But unless you forgive, you will continue to be tied to the wages of the sin. Your death will not teach him a lesson, nor will it set the record straight. You can only be free from it by choosing to forgive. Are you willing to do that now?"

"No!" she said emphatically. "After all he has done to me, it's not right that I should have to forgive him, too."

We continued to talk and pray together for a while, but Tina would not be comforted or consoled. Her bitterness was deep and she could not imagine releasing it. The irony is that she has a loving heart, which was evidenced by her heroic fight for her marriage all those years. However, the pain had turned her heart to stone.

I closed our time together by praying a blessing over her in which I asked the Holy Spirit to be her Comforter, and that she would find rest for her soul through Him.

Tina did not accept my invitation to come back for prayer. I heard from a mutual acquaintance that her health continued to decline and the chronic pain caused her to be increasingly bitter and lonely.

Betrayal is an attack against identity. Tina was a fun-loving girl with a loving heart, but she became a sour old woman unable to love because of the horrific betrayal she experienced. If she had been willing to forgive and release, it might not have changed Craig's heart, but it would have taken away her bitterness and left vengeance up to the Lord.

Chapter Twelve:
Fear and Anger

We destroy arguments and every lofty opinion raised against the knowledge of God, and take every thought captive to obey Christ. - 2 Corinthians 10:5

Pretensions, or "lofty opinions," are thoughts and ideas that are contrary to the knowledge of God. They come from lies or deceptions passed along from the devil, the father of lies, or they arise when our interpretation of events causes us to draw false conclusions. These pretensions are not true, but they form our paradigm, or worldview, and guide us.

People experience some unpleasant emotions, such as fear, anger, sadness, disgust, shame and hopelessness. A healthy person has learned to return to joy from these feelings, but when they persist it indicates the presence of a lofty opinion. Emotions are neither good nor bad but are a response to what we believe to be true. We "take every thought captive" by asking what the person believes that causes them to feel a certain way. We "make the thought obey Christ" by comparing their belief to what God reveals as His truth. The person is transformed, or healed, when God replaces the old belief, or lofty opinion, with His truth.

Chronic Fear

I sought the LORD, and He answered me and delivered me from all my fears. - Psalm 34:4

Fear is an unpleasant emotion caused by the belief that someone or something is dangerous, likely to cause pain, or a threat. This intense emotion overrides reason and initiates an immediate fight or flight response. Fear may be experienced in varying intensities, but it should be a temporary condition.

Chronic fear causes problems because it stimulates the stress hormones adrenalin and cortisol. The adrenal gland produces hormones that regulate blood volume and pressure, digestion and metabolism rates, suppression of the immune system and anti-inflammatory effects. The body responds with extra strength and intensity for a short period of time when triggered by fear but is not designed to maintain that condition. Harmful effects, such as adrenal fatigue, are symptomatic of chronic fear or its conditions.

The goal is not to avoid fear, nor deny its presence, but to appropriately resolve the root cause and then return to joy.

The prayer strategy for fear, as succinctly stated by David above, is to seek the LORD and let His answer deliver from all one's fears.

1) *Identify the object of fear.*
2) *Interrogate: What do you believe to be true to cause you to feel this way?*
3) *How did you come to believe this?*
4) *What does God have to say about this belief?*

The Object of Fear

Fear is an appropriate emotional response when the object of fear is a clear and present danger. In other words, an accurately identified threat should trigger fear and cause the person to respond with a fight or flight strategy. For example, the approach of an erratic stranger should put me on high alert. Not knowing his intentions, but realizing they could include my harm, is a clear and present danger.

Most threats of this nature are resolved in a moment. The erratic stranger passes by without a glance, for instance, and the presumed threat vanishes, or the stranger advances and you quickly step into a busy restaurant to evade the threat. Boundaries and limits are established to avoid danger that cannot be permanently resolved in another way.

Sometimes the object of fear is presumed or anticipated rather than a clear and present danger. Such residual fears can linger from an historic danger, which may have been very real and even caused pain but is no longer a current threat. The memory of the danger may still trigger a fear response. For instance, a driver who has survived a traumatic car accident may experience residual fear while approaching a similar intersection because of the prior experience.

— Learn from Me —

Carla had suffered for months from whiplash. She had looked up at her rearview mirror just in time to see a sedan bearing down on her too quickly to stop. The distracted driver noticed the red light too late and slammed into Carla's car and pushed her into oncoming traffic. The cars were totaled and the physical recovery had been slow.

"Have you forgiven the driver that hit you?" I asked.

"I never thought about it," answered Carla. "Since it was an accident, it didn't cross my mind. But now that you ask the question, I realize that I have been holding something against the young lady. I've been offended that she was paying attention to her phone instead of her driving."

I led her in prayer and acted as witness to the forgiveness, then followed up with a prayer of blessing and request for complete healing in Carla's neck. A few weeks later she sent me a text message that her neck was completely healed! Not only that, but she was no longer afraid to drive.

Carla experienced physical and emotional healing. She was set free from a presumptive fear of driving. The object of her fear was the memory of the accident. It is reasonable to want to avoid an accident, but she had become hyper-vigilant because of trauma she had experienced. She assigned "real and present danger" status to an historic event in an attempt to protect herself from a repeat experience. Once she was set free from that fear she was able to drive with an appropriate level of caution.

A person who uses fear as a tool for control may become the object of fear to the one being abused. For example, the devil uses the fear of death to hold people in bondage (Hebrews 2:14-15), but in so doing he becomes the thing to be feared. An abuser overrides the free will of another, and some people control by wielding fear, either directly or implied. The victim complies with the demands of the abuser under threat of danger or pain.

At first the object of fear is the pain of physical abuse, but when a pattern has been established the abusive person becomes the object of fear. He or she may no longer need to strike the victim to get obedience, instead the threat of violence is a clear and present danger.

One of the insidious aspects of fear occurs when the devil tempts a person to fear "fear" itself. This creates a vicious cycle of escalating fear that moves past anxiety and into panic, as described in the example of Martin in the first chapter.

The prayer strategy begins with identifying the object of fear, which helps the fearful one to focus on the perceived or real threat. Then through prayer we can explore what the person believes that gives the fear power.

Fear of Death

... That through death He might destroy the one who has the power of death, that is, the devil, and deliver all those who through fear of death were subject to lifelong slavery. – Hebrews 2:14-15

Many forms of fear find their origin in the truth that "the wages of sin is death (Romans 6:23)." The devil has the power of death and uses it to hold people in lifelong slavery through their fear of death. The unbeliever has an obvious reason for fear of death since it combines the fear of the unknown with an impending sense of the Judgment Day. Believers should be exempt from this leverage, but the devil uses accusation and shame to trigger fear even in some who have accepted eternal life and been redeemed.

Fear of pain is a fear of the dying process. In Hebrews 9:27 it says "it is appointed for man to die once, and after that comes judgment." Pain is a practical reminder of sin and that we are dying. Whereas pain seems to be the object of fear, the deeper root may be the fear of death. Once the fear of death is resolved, the devil has no more leverage over us.

Fear of rejection is a fear of the death of identity or personhood. We are created as relational beings to operate in community, and we get feedback about our identity from others. Rejection cuts off that source of information and we are left guessing about who we are. Once we know our identity in Christ, the fear of rejection has no basis.

Fear of betrayal, similarly, is a fear of the death of our rights and death of relationship. We are created with a free will and the expression of that is our right to choose. Betrayal occurs when someone else makes a choice for their benefit that harms us, and the offense of that betrayal kills relationship. Once we truly die to our self and choose to surrender our rights, the fear of betrayal holds no threat and has no power over us.

Fear of abandonment is also a form of death of community. We are dependent creatures, designed to serve the God that protects and provides for us. Abandonment leaves us with the belief that we must protect and provide for ourselves. Once we accept God's promise that He will never leave us or forsake us, and recognize Him as our Protector and Provider, the fear of abandonment is resolved.

Fear of failure is a prevalent fear of the death of reputation. We often call this "fear of man" because it is to fear the opinion of others. Once we accept that we can control our integrity but our reputation is assigned to us by others, then we can release the responsibility for protecting our reputation. The fear of failure then has no basis.

Fear of failure can also stem from a fear of the death of our expectations and dreams. These hopes and aspirations form our preferred future reputation, which we may fail to achieve. Once we put all our hope in the Lord our future is secure with Him and the fear of failure can no longer exist.

Fear of discovery is a fear of the death of innocence. This fear operates where there is hidden sin, or any cause for guilt, and threatens embarrassment or shame. Righteousness replaces innocence through forgiveness. Once we have received this forgiveness there is no threat of embarrassment or shame and we are no longer subject to the fear of discovery.

Sources of Chronic Fear

Your prayer strategy is guided when you know the source of fear. However, since we are complex creatures the fear may originate in one realm but soon affect each of the other realms as well, particularly when fear is chronic. For instance, a spirit of fear in the spiritual realm may incite habitual worry that upsets a chemical balance over time. We pray for healing at the root level and can expect the other realms to realign as the healing progresses.

Fear creeps into the spiritual realm because of sin committed by or against a person. For instance, fear used as a tool for control is a form of idolatry. When I use fear to control others I am placing myself in the position of God, requiring them to fear me. If I use fear for self-control I am replacing God with fear as my object of worship and service.

We use spiritual warfare to deal with demons and unclean spirits. Authority is given to us over these evil spirits by Jesus Christ, and in His Name we are able to cast them out. It is helpful to use the demon's name, such as "spirit of fear," "spirit of anxiety," or "spirit of the fear of man."

— Learn from Me —

Marcus was a good, hard working man, but suffered from fear of man. No matter how diligent he was, there was a nagging fear that he would not measure up to the expectations of others. His fear was particularly acute when he was around other Christians. He was a missionary kid who grew up in a developing culture where idolatry was rampant and superstitions abounded. His parents shielded him from the demonstrative aspects of delivery ministry and spiritual warfare, but he was not completely unaware of the battles.

We prayed together and asked God to reveal the source of his fear of man. Immediately he recalled the night his parents were away at the church conducting a prayer meeting. He was in his early teens and began to wonder about the power of the evil one. Suddenly he felt a cold wind blow right through him and he was terrified. He reasoned that a hidden sin gave a demon permission to oppress him, and he kept the experience to himself because of shame.

"Do you still experience that terror, or a similar emotion?" I asked.

"Yes, fairly regularly," he answered. "Most often it comes when I feel judged by others in the church. I know I can't live up to their expectations. It feels like I have to hide or I will be exposed to ridicule and shame. I'll feel it coming on during the day, but at night it can be unbearable."

"Would you be willing to ask God to forgive you for that hidden sin?" I asked.

"I don't know how, because I don't really know what that sin is," he confessed.

"God knows everything, right?" I asked. He nodded, and I continued, "And even if a sin is hidden, it is hidden from you, not Him. Couldn't you confess it as a hidden sin, and let Him fill in the blanks?"

"I never thought of it that way before, but of course that will work!"

He confessed the sin while I acted as witness to the spiritual transaction. I asked him if he would like to be free from that spirit of fear and he readily agreed.

"Spirit of the fear of man, you are not welcome here. You have no right to be here, and we command you to leave in the name of Jesus, and never return!" I said firmly.

"I just felt a warm sense of peace inside me!" Marcus shared. "It seemed to start right in my chest and expand from there. That demon is totally gone now, isn't it?"

I confirmed it and we offered a prayer of thanksgiving for his new freedom from fear. Several months later he mentioned to me that he no longer frets over the opinions of others and is able to work just for the glory of God

Chronic fear can also originate in the emotional realm. Stress is habitual and many people have become accustomed to its presence. The root of the stress is excess responsibility, either assigned or assumed, that the person is unable to manage. Stress tends to inflate a risk, and it gives way to worry. Worry is to think about a problem for which you have no solution. Worry then escalates to anxiety which involves the whole body in the problem. Anxiety ultimately gives way to panic in which fear takes over the person's identity by overriding reason and function.

The prayer strategy to overcome fear, at any of these levels of expression, is to discover the source of stress or responsibility. We know that God has all power, knowledge and authority and is the only One who can assume all responsibility. When the person receives forgiveness for taking on responsibility that is not his or hers to take it opens the door for release. If the responsibility has been assigned by someone else, that person needs to be forgiven as well.

Some people live with the constant threat of rejection, betrayal, abandonment or other phobias. These fears can be interrogated for truth and released through forgiveness. Remember that the object of the fear, which is the threat, is resolved when God renews the person's mind.

— *Learn from Me* —

For instance, a woman grew up in a household where she was left on her own from an early age. As she demonstrated the ability to survive on her own, her parents were gone more often. They threw themselves into their careers, blew off steam with entertainment, and spent less and less time at home. Their daughter learned to cope with the isolation but lived with the nagging fear that her parents would one day abandon her altogether.

She married, partly in the hope that she would never be at risk of abandonment again. Her husband was attracted to her independence and relished the freedom to pursue his work and hobbies. However, they never grew close and soon the fear of abandonment she had toward her parents was transferred to him. Their lifestyle, while enjoyable on one level, perpetuated her fear.

God revealed her chronic fear of abandonment through prayer and she confessed her sin that she did not trust Him as provider and protector. She forgave her parents for feeding that fear, and then followed up by forgiving her husband. As the fear of abandonment ceased, she felt a heart of worship grow within her. She recognized the gift of worship as God's proof that He had healed the fear and replaced it with faith in Him.

Physical conditions can trigger fear, anxiety and panic. For instance, a chemical imbalance can trigger the amygdala which creates a heightened sense of fear and anxiety that produces a fight-or-flight response for the sake of survival. This can happen with hormonal shifts in a changing body or as the result of drugs. A well-known culprit is methamphetamine, a drug that creates a release of dopamine in the reward centers of the brain. The meth user overtaxes the body's ability to produce dopamine and then experiences unfocused anxiety, a sense of danger, and paranoia as a result.

Current research suggests that some panic attacks may be triggered by elevated levels of carbon dioxide in the blood stream.[4] This results in "false suffocation alarms" initiating fight-for-survival fear and anxiety.[5] The symptoms of this fear are no different than those initiated in the spiritual or emotional realms, but the solution is quite simple: breathe deeply and let your lungs exchange oxygen for carbon dioxide in your blood vessels.

When the root cause of fear is physical, the first place to find solution is the physical realm. Hunger can trigger strong emotions, such as anger and fear. Sleep deprivation symptoms include moodiness, including fear. Adrenal fatigue can both lead to or be caused by chronic fear.

Allow your prayer strategy to consider spiritual, emotional and physical sources for fear. Ask the Holy Spirit to guide the process and pursue healing at the root level. Fear is an unpleasant emotion, and the temptation is to accept any temporary relief as a cure. Rather than settle for symptom relief, use the opportunity of reduced fear to dig into its source. Then the healing will be complete and the symptoms eradicated.

Peace Will Guard Your Heart

Let your reasonableness be known to everyone. The Lord is at hand; do not be anxious about anything, but in everything by prayer and supplication with thanksgiving let your requests be made known to God. And the peace of God, which surpasses all understanding, will guard your hearts and your minds in Christ Jesus. - Philippians 4:5-7

This scripture often comes up when we have a prayer appointment that deals with fear. First, we are commanded to let our reasonableness be known to everyone. Fear substitutes urgency and action (fight or flight) in place of reasonableness, so resolving fear is essential in the Christian walk. Second, the Lord is at hand. His presence is the antidote to abandonment and all the other objects of chronic fear. Third, do not be anxious about anything. Faith in God as Provider and gratitude for all He has done is the solution for anxiousness. Finally, the peace of God will guard our hearts and minds in Christ Jesus.

This last sentence elicits a mental image of a sentry stationed over your heart and mind. Many people post a sentry of fear, which is the world's way of guarding against threats. Fear controls your heart, which is the core of your identity. Fear overrides your mind, which is your paradigm and frame of reference. When fear is the sentry of your heart and mind, fear is multiplied because it increases fear.

The passage in Philippians, however, urges us to place the peace of God as sentry over our heart and mind. This is the promised outcome of releasing anxiety and worry for the sake of His presence. The peace that takes the place of fear is beyond our ability to understand, but we know it when we experience it. Each person gets to choose which sentry they want, and under duress they may have chosen fear. When they choose peace, I invite them to "fire" fear by terminating the employment contract.

— Learn from Me —

Betty grew up in a chaotic household. Her parents were alcoholics and her siblings rebelled against all forms of authority. As the most sensitive of the children, she took it upon herself to create order and maintain some semblance of normalcy. It was an impossible task and her health suffered under the self-assigned responsibility.

She was quick to confess that she had taken on responsibility that was not hers to take, and she received forgiveness. I asked God if there was anything else standing in the way of her complete healing.

"Fear," was her one-word answer.

"Lord, could you give us some clarification about this fear?" I prayed.

"He showed me that I use fear to control and protect myself," she explained. "I know it's true, because fear has been such a constant companion ever since I was a child. Honestly, I'm not sure I know how to manage my life without it."

She went on to describe her habit of assuming the worst, preparing for catastrophe, and operating under a worst-case scenario. She agreed that it made her more cautious than others but shared some examples of how disaster was averted because of her planning. She was convinced that such risk management was only reasonable.

"Do you realize you are guarding your heart with fear?" I asked. "While you have some evidence of success, the truth is that you continue to have fear as your constant companion. I believe your complete healing will include freedom from fear."

I then opened my Bible to the passage in Philippians and shared about the two sentries. She agreed in prayer as I asked God to make the exchange. Then I asked her to repeat after me:

"Spirit of fear, you have been guarding my heart for a long time, but you have been doing a lousy job. You're fired. Pack up your belongings and leave. Peace of God, you're the new guard of my heart and mind. Welcome aboard."

Anger and Rage

Know this, my beloved brothers: let every person be quick to hear, slow to speak, slow to anger; for the anger of man does not produce the righteousness of God. - James 1:19-20

Anger is an unpleasant emotion of annoyance, displeasure or hostility. It prepares you for a fight-or-flight response, just as the emotion of fear does, and it is triggered by something you believe to be true. Anger is a strong emotion that demands a response.

Anger is an expressive emotion. It often gives voice for a companion emotion that is deemed unsafe or unwise to display. For instance, in an environment where there is a constant battle for control a person may believe it is unwise to show fear which might demonstrate vulnerability. In such cases anger may be displayed in fear's place to protect a presumed position of power.

Chronic anger is a powerful emotion that should have short duration and be quickly resolved. That is why Paul wrote: "Be angry and do not sin; do not let the sun go down on your anger (Ephesians 4:26)." Anger puts a body on "high alert," which is counterproductive to a good night's sleep. Not only that, but the body responds to the chemical signals and physiological changes even when an enemy is not there to fight. In the absence of an enemy, the body begins to fight against itself in a way that causes distress and leads to disease.

The goal is not to avoid anger, nor to suppress it or mask its message, but to appropriately resolve the root cause and then return to joy.

The prayer strategy for anger is to consider how you have used anger in the past, identify its triggers, discover any companion emotions, and then interrogate what you believe to be true that causes you to feel this way. The anger is resolved when we discover the truth and release the cause of anger to God.

1) *Identify the trigger of anger.*
2) *Check for companion emotions.*
3) *Interrogate: What do you believe to be true to cause you to feel this way?*
4) *How did you come to believe this?*
5) *Who needs to be forgiven for causing you to believe this?*
6) *Examine: What does God have to say about this belief?*

God has quite a bit to say about anger, and a few very well-known verses summarize His opinion on the matter:

But I say to you that everyone who is angry with his brother will be liable to judgment ... - Matthew 5:22

Refrain from anger, and forsake wrath! Fret not yourself; it tends only to evil. - Psalm 37:8

Let all bitterness and wrath and anger and clamor and slander be put away from you, along with all malice. - Ephesians 4:31

In summary, anger against your brother is akin to murder, anger tends only to evil, and these statements include anger in all its forms or expressions. Although people have experienced anger in many different forms, it is helpful for them to understand their anger style so they can confess and repent its inappropriate use. We describe anger by its characteristics using three different styles: Flash Point, Pressure Cooker, and Crock Pot.

Learn from Me

Flash Point Anger

Flash Point Anger comes in a sudden eruption and without warning, which is why this style of anger is so hard to control. A person may present a calm and cool temperament and live in that condition most of the time, but then something triggers anger and there is an explosion.

The Flash Point Anger person struggles to control these outbursts. Often it elicits denial: "Where did that come from? That's not who I am: I'm calm and cool." Denial may be followed with a renewed cycle of resolve, trigger, failure and guilt. It is not impossible to discover the root of Flash Point Anger, but first the person must accept the truth that he or she has it.

— Learn from Me —

I have some experience with Flash Point Anger because of my childhood. I am fifth of eight preacher's kids. My dad had this style of anger, and sometimes when we misbehaved he would completely lose his temper. Usually it was expressed verbally, with loud words, sometimes in Dutch. We all knew what it meant, though: "I'm in trouble."

I also have some experience with Flash Point Anger because of my young adulthood. I was an easy-going, fun-loving person almost all of the time. Except, every once in a while, I would explode in anger, usually with a verbal assault. It was a behavior I learned from my dad.

It is no surprise that my dad acquired this style of anger. He was fourteen years old when the Germans occupied his homeland, The Netherlands. He lived through the Second World War as a teenager, amid constant threat and danger. In his later years he was healed from the constant vigilance and trauma of the war, but as a young father he still carried the triggers.

My healing from Flash Point Anger came through prayer, identifying the perceived threat, forgiving my father for demonstrating the power of sudden eruptions, and breaking off a generational curse. The turning point came when I accepted the fact that I was not a calm and cool person that sometimes blew up, but that I was a Flash Point anger man in need of healing.

Pressure Cooker Anger

Pressure Cooker Anger is a suppressed emotional response to past offenses or events. The anger builds up pressure inside the person but is constrained. The outward appearance belies the seething response, unless the lid blows off. If pressure cooker anger explodes it can ruin your kitchen.

The Pressure Cooker Anger person is aware of his or her anger issue but is under the impression that it is controlled. The seeds of anger typically go back to an original offense, and then over time similar forms of anger are added to it. A current event triggers an exaggerated response for a moment, then the lid is clamped back on and the new anger is added to the former anger inside the pressure cooker.

Pressure cookers come equipped with a safety valve to let steam escape if the pressure gets too high. This is the source of the word picture: "letting off a little steam." Additionally, the pressure cooker anger person is likely to exhibit some false escape valves. These are behaviors or strategies that let off some of the pressure without blowing up the kitchen.

The escape valve allows a manageable amount of anger to be expressed, or a sense of justice displayed, which fulfills the purpose of the pent-up anger. For example, some may vicariously vent through action movies, thrillers, westerns, and violent sports. Others may engage in mean-spirited gossip, sarcasm, or crime shows for the same reason. Anything that allows anger to safely be expressed can act as this escape valve, but it does not truly resolve the anger constrained inside.

Holding anger in this manner causes physical distress which leads to diseases, such as hypertension, heart issues, digestive problems, insomnia, and more. Anger can also cause emotional distress because energy is reserved for anger and not available for pleasant emotions. A root of bitterness, which often accompanies pent up anger, is like poison to the body.

— *Learn from Me* —

Kyle lacked some social graces and motivation as he grew up because his parents worked a lot. His classmates picked on him for being plump and a little undisciplined, and this was a great source of rejection to him. When someone called him a name, pushed him around, or ignored him it hurt deeply, but Kyle did not retaliate for fear it would lead to further rejection. He suppressed it.

He experienced rejection from coworkers when he began his career, and each time it added a little more anger to the pile. Soon the pressure cooker was full and he had difficulty keeping it under control. He hated his job but had to work. He lashed out at sports commentators, talk show hosts, and other "safe" targets. His family feared for their safety on the chance that his escape valve would one day fail and all the anger would spew out at them.

Kyle was surprised to discover that the root of his anger was rejection, but God had been very clear about it as we prayed. I invited him to forgive the boys that had rejected him; his parents for being absent; and his co-workers for adding to the offense. He felt something truly release as he let the offenses go and he allowed the peace of God to fill the void.

Crock Pot Anger

A crock pot rarely boils over but spends most of its time on a steady low heat. Managing anger becomes a normal way of life for the crock pot person. As long as the temperature is low they let it stew, but if it starts to rise up they take some action to bring it back under control.

Unlike the pressure cooker, a crock pot is easily monitored by others as well. The people around the Crock Pot Anger person are well aware of the state of anger. When the temperature rises they are likely to slip away or mollify, to do whatever it takes to maintain the status quo.

In Crock Pot Anger, a person stews over an original root of bitterness and similar ingredients are easily added. For instance, if the initial offense is an act of betrayal then subsequent acts or threats of betrayal become additional proof of offense. The root of bitterness grows and the anger response is amplified along with it.

Chronic anger is the norm for this temperament, and the coping strategies are subtle and generally associated with a companion emotion. For example, if fear is the companion emotion then the coping strategy will likely fall along the lines of fight-or-flight. A person who feels his temperature rising may escape to an isolated place to compose himself, which is a polite expression of a flight response. Along that line, he may escape into video gaming, fantasy, or other alternate reality situations.

Nevertheless, the root of bitterness and chronic anger cause distress inside the person, which causes conflict that escalates into disease. Some symptoms of this style of anger are digestive issues, ulcers, autoimmune diseases, and certain forms of cancer.

— Learn from Me —

Paul was placed in a position of authority at work but struggled to perform his duties at his normally high standard. It was a stretch for him to take on the new role, and he feared that he would not measure up in the eyes of his board. It was a nagging fear that he felt in his prior job as well, but he believed it went with the territory.

Whenever staff members under-performed, Paul would take them to task because of how it might reflect on him. He would not yell, but when he spoke harshly it was just as effective. He felt bad about the bruised relationships and would try to make amends, but then the cycle would repeat.

Paul and I prayed about his management style, and the Lord revealed the connection between his anger and his fear of man. We interrogated that emotion and he was reminded of the spiritual leader who had first made him feel inferior. We engaged in a spiritual transaction of forgiveness and Paul was able to release the fear and accompanying anger. He was delighted to discover in the next few months that his "nervous stomach" had been healed as well.

Companion Emotions

Anger can express a companion emotion such as fear, guilt, embarrassment, or disgust. In our prayer strategy we interrogate an emotion to discover the underlying belief. Although anger is the presenting emotion, we may need to identify and interrogate the companion emotion to get to the root issue. This is particularly true when anger masks or overshadows the companion emotion.

Some companion emotions precede the anger response while others follow. As mentioned earlier, I had a flash point anger problem as a young man. If I felt someone disapproved of me, especially if I was falsely accused of wrong, I would become embarrassed, and that embarrassment would quickly escalate to explosive anger. I had to interrogate the embarrassment to discover the underlying belief because anger was a tool I used to hide my embarrassment.

— Learn from Me —

I prayed with Phil about anger issues and we could not find the root. There was no discernable pattern to his outbursts of anger and no known trigger. We asked for guidance in prayer and initially nothing new came to his mind.

"Phil, what are you afraid of?" I asked.

"I'm not afraid of anything!" he answered with confidence. Phil was a big man and had a history of getting his way by force.

"No, really ... what are you afraid of?" I asked again.

"My wife," he answered quietly, as if it were a new thought.

"Your wife? Your little wife? You're afraid of your wife?" I blurted out in an unguarded way.

"I really am!" he said with a tone of wonder in his voice. Then he added, "I'm afraid she'll leave me."

Immediately I knew Phil's companion emotion was fear of rejection as a response to his belief that she might leave him. We interrogated that belief, and asked God to give truth in its place.

God showed him that no matter what, He was enough. A new sense of peace and hope came over Phil, and he let go of the fear. His heart opened up in a new way toward his wife and he was excited to see how their relationship would change.

Phil overcame anger that day. More importantly, our prayer time went to the root of the problem, which was his fear of rejection. God often resolves the root problem to fix the presenting symptom.

Triggers

It is helpful to discover the triggers that cause someone to express anger. First, we want to explore the physical factors that can initiate an anger episode. These are generally things that can be controlled once they are known. For instance, some people are susceptible to anger when they are hungry or their blood sugar level is low, and people have begun to use the term "hangry" to describe this condition. When that is known, anger can be averted with a good meal or protein bar.

Other common physical triggers are sleep deprivation, hormonal imbalance or changes, certain situational triggers, and chemically induced reactions. Some drugs, prescription and otherwise, have a side effect of triggering anger.

Emotional triggers, particularly companion emotions, can lead to anger or follow it. Watching for a triggering emotion can help build your prayer strategy and inform you of the emotion and belief that must be interrogated.

Learn from Me

Spiritual triggers can come from demonic influence, possession, or oppression. A spirit of anger can gain control over a person by invitation or deception. These spirits can also arise from curses or as consequences of unforgiven sin. For example, an individual with uncontrollable outbursts of anger may require spiritual warfare to be set free from the oppressive spirits.

— Learn from Me —

Brandon struggled with outbursts of anger and felt bad when he intimidated people with his large presence and big voice. He said he rarely lost his temper but sometimes he spoke with too much intensity. I asked him to clarify, so he raised his voice to demonstrate. I was frightened.

"How do you distinguish between speaking with too much intensity and losing your temper?" I asked.

"Well, I'm verbal," he answered. "I don't lose my temper and hit anyone, but I do speak my mind."

"Let me recommend that we consider both expressions as a demonstration of anger, whether you are speaking your mind or losing your temper. Would you be willing to ask God to heal you from this anger?"

He quickly agreed, so we asked God to reveal the trigger of his anger.

"Oh, it happens when someone disagrees with me," he said.

"When someone disagrees with you, how does that make you feel? I mean, besides the anger response, what other feeling do you have in that situation?" I asked.

"This is strange, but it makes me feel isolated, alone, like I've been set aside," he answered thoughtfully.

"Let's take that to prayer," I said, and then I continued aloud in prayer: "Lord, would you show Brandon what he believes to be true that causes him to feel isolated or alone?"

"I believe that my opinion doesn't matter," he replied.

Continuing in prayer, I asked, "Lord, Brandon believes in these situations that his opinion doesn't matter. Would you reveal to him how he came to believe this?"

"My dad, when he was home, was verbally abusive. When I was a kid he would yell at me for something, and when I tried to explain he wouldn't listen. I was willing to take his anger when I was in the wrong, but many times he yelled at me for something I didn't do. He just wouldn't listen to me. No matter what I thought, it didn't matter to him."

"Isn't it interesting that even now as an adult, when it feels like your opinion doesn't matter, you raise your voice in an attempt to be heard?" I observed. "Would you be willing to forgive your dad for not giving you a voice and for rejecting your opinions?"

I acted as a witness for the spiritual transaction as he forgave his dad for rejecting his opinions and several other offenses that came to his mind. He gave a huge sigh of relief as he released the offenses and looked at me expectantly.

I prayed, "Lord, Brandon has forgiven his dad for not allowing him to have an opinion or defend himself. Please reveal to him what he needs to know about the belief that his opinion doesn't matter."

"I just had a mental image of Jesus listening to me. It was like He was standing near me, just waiting for me to talk. He wants me to share my heart with Him!" Brandon exclaimed.

Brandon was set free that day from outbursts of anger. Even when people disagreed with his point of view he was not triggered into loudly defending his position. Rather than be boisterous and bullying he is now free to passionately express his heart without intimidating others.

Chapter Thirteen:
Disgust and Shame

Then Rebekah said to Isaac, "I loathe my life because of the Hittite women. If Jacob marries one of the Hittite women like these, one of the women of the land, what good will my life be to me?" - Genesis 27:46

Disgust is an unpleasant emotional response of revulsion to something considered offensive, distasteful, or unpleasant. It helps protect and maintain purity, morality, boundaries, principles, and values. However, chronic disgust can lead to anxiety disorders or cause someone to be dissatisfied and impossible to please.

The disgust response is signaled through facial expressions and body language. The eyebrows arch up in the middle, the nose wrinkles and the mouth forms a pout; so our language includes the idiom "turn up our nose" to indicate disgust. The body language is generally followed by actions of avoidance or withdrawal. For instance, plugging the nose or covering the eyes are forms of removing oneself from an offensive thing. In general, greater disgust is accompanied with more dramatic signals. These signals express the emotion of disgust and communicate it to others.

Physical elicitors of disgust tend to be associated with perceived health risks, such as disease, infection, poor hygiene, or other dangers. For example, arachnophobia is an extreme disgust of spiders due to fear of personal harm. Similarly, a disgust response toward rats or other vermin is rooted in the fear of transmitted diseases. These physical elicitors can serve to protect health for the individual and community.

Emotional elicitors of disgust tend to be associated with moral risks, such as antisocial behavior or demonstrations of immorality. For example, people feel revulsion toward murder or physical or verbal abuse. These emotional elicitors can serve to protect the morality of an individual and community.

The opposite of disgust is trust. The one who properly operates in disgust becomes confident in physical and moral purity, which leads to trust.

Desensitized Disgust

They have become callous and have given themselves up to sensuality, greedy to practice every kind of impurity. - Ephesians 4:19

The biggest problem with desensitized disgust is the lack of guidance for moral purity. The Apostle Paul describes this condition as becoming callous, in the scripture above, or having a seared conscience. The lack of guidance leaves them vulnerable to impurity and all its consequences.

One of the primary causes of desensitization is repeated exposure. For example, the one who works in a rendering plant or meatpacking plant becomes insensitive to death, decay, and other indications of health danger. They must ignore or turn off their olfactory senses and association between death and disease. Rejecting the response begins as an intentional process but once they become callous it continues automatically. We see similar incidents of desensitization by people who become callous to horror films, pornography, and debauchery of any kind.

An attitude or tolerance in a society leads the way to cultural desensitization. When a person first experiences the wages of sin they are disgusted, but when society demands that they accept all behavior as valid it serves to sear the conscience. Not only does this lack of disgust allow others to sin without being confronted, but it also erodes the individual's personal guide for moral purity. The opposite of disgust is not acceptance but trustworthy moral purity.

Desensitized disgust is dehumanizing both to self and others. It removes the guide that keeps us from harm and allows others to fall into the trap of immorality as well.

The solution for a desensitized standard for disgust is to repent and accept God's standards for holy living. We must allow ourselves to be disgusted with sin and evil just as God is. However, while you preserve your pure conscience and tender heart make sure that you release to God all responsibility for judging sin and evil.

— Learn from Me —

Marcus recalled the rush of excitement and danger he felt when he came across a stash of pornographic magazines in his dad's dresser drawer. There was a twinge of guilt when he looked at the pictures, but his eight-year-old curiosity was piqued and he sneaked in whenever he could. By the time he was a teen he had accumulated his own stash, stolen from the local convenience store. His over-exposure expanded in his adult years with internet access and digital media. He was never far removed from access.

He came for prayer at his wife's request. His addiction was a source of great disgust and disappointment to her but he was unable to be free from it. He had a dirty mind, wandering eye, and disregard for women. He wanted to make a change but had no power to do so. All the filters, accountability partners, and Bible studies were not effective, either. He was nearly out of hope.

We went to prayer. God had reminded Marcus of the root of the problem, so I invited him to forgive his dad and mom for not protecting his innocence. Before doing so, he wanted to confess his part of the sin, particularly how he incorporated it into his life from childhood to adulthood. I acted as witness to these spiritual transactions. Then I asked God to restore him with a mind of purity toward nakedness and intimacy.

Marcus reported back a little later that he had been set free from the compulsion and temptation of pornography, but he was even more excited to share how his view of his wife had changed. His tendency to compare and judge had fallen away and he was filled with a new sense of love and admiration for her. God had restored him with a healthy sense of disgust and given him a new mind.

Moral Hypervigilance

Beloved, never avenge yourselves, but leave it to the wrath of God, for it is written, "Vengeance is mine, I will repay, says the Lord." - Romans 12:19

The opposite of desensitized disgust is moral hypervigilance. Chronic disgust can become judgmental and condemning, defending one's self-imposed standard rather than acting as a moral guide. The hypervigilant person is disgusted with any conviction, opinion, or action that conflicts with his ideals. He becomes susceptible to taking responsibility for the morality of others in a way that far exceeds his authority.

Hypervigilance leads to chronic dissatisfaction. The person with this over-developed sense of morality is impossible to please because no one can measure up to the standards he defines and defends.

The source of moral hypervigilance may be cultural or the result of a generational curse through people groups or families that practice extreme disgust responses. Elevating one's convictions can also lead to moral high ground and hypocrisy because the standards are unachievable.

— Learn from Me —

Tom was a self-described hot-head. He engaged in road rage and was impatient with everyone. The slightest thing would set him off and send him out of control. He was bitter and frustrated most of the time. His wife had encouraged him to get help.

We began by asking God to show him what he was believing that caused him to get angry.

"When I see someone do something wrong it really makes me mad," he said. "I try to not make a big deal over it, but I can't ignore it. I mean, how can I just let it go?"

"Why don't you ask God why this is so important to you?" I suggested, and Tom quickly agreed.

"God said I'm a self-appointed sheriff!" Tom said with a laugh.

He went on to describe how he had grown up in a strict home where any infraction was punished. He had great respect for the law and commandments and had tried to keep them perfectly. Anyone who did less was offensive to him.

Tom apologized to God for impersonating an officer and received forgiveness. His face broke into a big smile as the weight of responsibility lifted from his shoulders. When we had broken off a generational curse of legalism he could imagine a freer life filled with joy.

Self-Disgust

Self-disgust is the belief that "I am disgusting" and leads to self-loathing, often related to shame. When this belief takes root, it creates a vicious cycle because the thought of impurity leads to disgust which in itself is disgusting. Self-disgust can arise from a shame-based family or community, self-discovered guilt, or an awareness of impurity without an accompanying solution.

Self-disgust often manifests as a critical spirit. The person with this trait will assuage himself by saying he is his own harshest critic, and that his criticism of you is for your own good or protection. You can replace the word criticism with disgust. Some forms of obsessive compulsive disorder (OCD) are rooted in this kind of self-disgust. It is dehumanizing and by its nature has become a faulty guide for purity.

True forgiveness from God is the only solution for self-disgust. The impurity that triggers disgust is abundantly obvious to the person and can be confessed as sin. Once forgiveness has been received, he can repent to God's standard of righteousness which comes by faith. There is no condemnation (disgust) for those who are in Christ Jesus (Romans 8:1).

Learn from Me

Prayer Strategy

It is right and normal to experience disgust. It is a God-given emotion that helps us protect purity in the physical and moral realms. However, a lack of disgust from a seared conscience must be healed. Similarly, a broken sense of disgust expressed outwardly or inwardly must be healed. Chronic disgust can lead to impurity, judgment, and an inability to return to joy.

 1) *Identify the disgust trigger (elicitor).*
 2) *Ask: What rules are being broken?*
 3) *Ask: Is the standard based on God's opinion or another's?*
 4) *Repent to God's ways (standards).*
 5) *Spiritual transaction: Forgive and / or be forgiven.*
 6) *Release responsibility and vengeance.*
 7) *Return to joy through trust.*

We identify the trigger to discover the real reason for disgust, which may come from the physical, emotional, or spiritual realms. Then we ask what rules are being broken, or what about this trigger indicates impurity. Legitimate disgust occurs when God's standards are disobeyed, but illegitimate disgust is based on a phantom standard.

Repent to God's ways by accepting His standards and being reconciled through forgiveness. Discover and eliminate the standards of our own imagination which diverge from God's ways. We engage in the spiritual transactions of forgiveness and being forgiven to open the way to identify and release the disgust. Then, as needed, we release ourselves from the responsibility over moral standards and vengeance for failures.

We must keep our attention on the purpose of disgust and allow our responses to be driven by purity. Beware of desensitized disgust through cultural influence or repeated exposure and watch for unreliable guides of disgust from our own frame of reference rather than from God's definition of purity. We will find our ability to trust Him increases as our sensitivity to His ways becomes more certain by use.

Shame

Shame is an unpleasant emotion caused by consciousness of guilt, shortcoming, or impropriety. Everyone experiences shame because "all have sinned and fallen short of the glory of God (Romans 3:23)." The expressions of shame are remorse, sorrow, embarrassment, disappointment, guilt, sadness, and depression. Disgust and shame respond to impurity similarly, but disgust is triggered by observing it outside of one's self whereas shame is triggered by the sin from within. Therefore, shame is a more personal response and has a stronger effect on identity.

The purpose of shame is to make one sorry for his sin so he asks for forgiveness and acts in repentance. A person's conscience and understanding of right and wrong form the basis for shame, and there seems to be an innate moral compass that affects the feelings of guilt and shame.

Shame was first experienced by Adam and Eve in the Garden of Eden. They were naked and unashamed before sin but immediately after sinning they hid their nakedness and withdrew from God. Shame leads to hiding, withdrawal, isolation, and separation. The godly response to shame is confession leading to forgiveness but the fleshly response is a "pretension" that sparks anger, self-justification, and blame shifting.

Chronic shame occurs when someone feels he has done wrong and is unable to reconcile the offense or change the record. He may respond with anger as a cover for the embarrassment that accompanies his feelings of guilt, or he may attempt to explain away the offense or justify his role in it.

Blame shifting is common with the onset of shame. Eve blamed the serpent and Adam blamed Eve, each in an attempt to remove shame. But blame shifting does not transfer blame, it multiplies it. In other words, you can try to give shame to someone else by blaming them, but even if they accept the blame you both end up with shame.

Learn from Me

Shame is often used as a tool to control others. Religions, cultures, social groups, and families may use shame-based relating to force compliance or manipulate others' choices. They create an environment that is hostile toward forgiveness and then use the threat or punishment of shame to control. These law-based relationships use the threat of shame as an incentive for compliance, and the permanent nature of shame as the punishment.

> *Wash me thoroughly from my iniquity, and cleanse me from my sin! For I know my transgressions, and my sin is ever before me.* - Psalm 51:2-3

Prayer Strategy

The only true solution to shame is forgiveness, through which we are reconciled to God through Christ Jesus (2 Corinthians 5:19). Once we accept forgiveness, God declares that we are guiltless and the reason for shame disappears. We are set free.

1) *Take an account of the offense(s).*
2) *Confess the sin to God.*
3) *Spiritual Transaction: receive forgiveness.*
4) *Check for any "deeds of repentance."*
5) *Ask God to reveal the truth in your renewed mind.*
6) *Live in the reconciled identity.*

Some people come for prayer completely aware of their shame. They have low self-esteem and expect to be rejected and abandoned. As King David wrote in Psalm 51, their sin (or shame) is ever before them. They carry their guilt like a huge weight and may be addicted to coping strategies. They are the easy ones to work with because they have a major sin issue or a laundry list of them.

Some people attempt to hide their shame from others and even from themselves. They exhibit hiding strategies, such as withdrawal, isolation, lying, an active fantasy life, or other forms of escapism. Others become perfectionists in an attempt to avoid reasons for shame. Still others revise history to put themselves in a better light, or to compulsively explain their motive or behavior.

For known or suspected shame issues, begin with a prayer that asks God to reveal the source of guilt or sin in the person's life. God may bring to mind the earliest experience of guilt, or the sin that caused the deepest remorse, or perhaps a representative sin from a pattern of behavior.

Take a thorough accounting of the offenses since forgiveness is the foundational step for removing shame. Follow the Holy Spirit's leading in this step. He may lead you to tackle the horrific sins first to get them out of the way, or He may allow you to warm up on what seems like lesser sins to build confidence to handle the tougher ones.

Pride is the most likely challenge that stands in the way of a person accepting forgiveness. The lies of pride fall into three categories when it comes to shame. The first type of pride asserts the ability to pay back the debt, but sin cannot be undone it must be forgiven. The second type is pride that claims one is too evil to be forgiven, which elevates the sin above the grace of God. Last is the pride that one does not deserve to be forgiven, which is a conclusion that God is too small to forgive or is constrained by the very laws He created.

— Learn from Me —

Joe hit bottom and asked God to help him overcome a twenty-year addiction to alcohol. I prayed that God would reveal the root of the problem.

"It's a lump of remorse," Joe explained. "I've had this lump of remorse inside me for as long as I can remember and the only way to cope with it is to be drunk. As soon as I sober up it hits me again."

"What are you remorseful about?"

"That I've wasted my life and that I've caused so much pain. I've caused pain to my family, my exes, my kids, and myself."

I invited Joe to ask God to forgive him for wasting his life and causing pain. He assured me that he had already tried that but he was willing to do it again. I acted as witness for the spiritual transaction as he received forgiveness and then asked how it made him feel.

"That's different," he said with a grin. Obviously, he was not a demonstrative man. "I don't know how you did that, but it feels different. I can feel my soul."

I explained that the change he felt was entirely divine and my role was strictly as witness. We talked about how his life will be impacted because the power of forgiveness changes the past rather than just forgetting it. He discovered the lump of remorse had been blocking his ability to feel his soul, but now that he had been forgiven the remorse was gone. Peace had taken its place!

— *Learn from Me* —

Gordon was consumed with shame. He was a missionary kid, raised in a strict Christian home, and everyone expected him to follow his father's footsteps. But he was crippled by a hidden sin of pornography. The shame plagued him until he finally faced it and admitted his problem to a support group. His confession made the shame increase all the more and he wondered if it had been a mistake to seek help. He was reluctant to share his burden with me, but his desperation to be free from shame was greater than his reluctance.

God quickly revealed the root of his pornography addiction so I invited Gordon to ask for forgiveness. He objected on the grounds that he had begged God for forgiveness regularly for more than thirty years and not received it. He was willing to try but had no faith it would be granted. I led him through the spiritual transaction but there was no breakthrough.

Something was blocking Gordon's forgiveness, so I asked God to reveal the barrier. Immediately Gordon recalled the moment he rejected God. At age fourteen, he intentionally blasphemed the Holy Spirit and willfully committed the unpardonable sin (Matthew 12:31-32). I asked if he would be willing to ask God to forgive that sin.

He looked at me quizzically, as if he could not decide if I was joking or doctrinally obtuse. He was leaning toward the latter.

"If you're willing, let's just ask God and let Him decide if He wants to forgive you or not," I suggested.

Much to Gordon's surprise and delight, God chose to forgive his rash act of rebellion. He wept as the truth filled him and washed away his shame. When I invited him to confess the sin that set him up for addiction he was quick to accept. God forgave and removed that source of shame and set him free. Then God gave him a vision of his true identity, and it was glorious.

— *Learn from Me* —

Audrey was married to a narcissist for thirty-two years. She was used to walking on eggshells as she grew up and had married George in part to escape the conflict in her home. He was charming, confident, and just what she needed to navigate through life. However, it was quickly obvious that George had shame issues. He could not admit a mistake and was a master at blame-shifting.

At first Audrey tried talking with George about the problems, but he would not engage. He would argue his point rather than listen and turned every confrontational conversation into a monologue. He used volume and velocity of words to override her interjections, and she learned not to argue or respond in any way lest the blizzard of words stretch on even longer. The message of his tirade was always the same: "You are to blame."

George must have been motivated by excruciating shame. It did not take long for Audrey to admit that she was part of the problem and had a share in the blame, but over the years she ultimately came to believe that everything was her fault. She lived in shame because her husband was wracked with it.

Through prayer, Audrey came to understand her guilt and was able to separate her role from the one assigned to her. She forgave George for the verbal abuse and blame-shifting. God gave her a new identity in Christ and she no longer needed someone to tell her who or what she was. She was free to be the woman God created her to be.

Chapter Fourteen:
Sadness and Hopelessness

You will be sorrowful, but your sorrow will turn into joy. -
John 16:20b

Sadness is an unpleasant emotion caused by feelings of loss, disadvantage, despair, grief, helplessness, disappointment, or sorrow. Sadness takes an account of loss so a person can recognize and accept what it has cost him or her. Once the debt has been acknowledged, the person who experienced the loss can choose to release it. This is the essence of the grieving process.

The person who experiences loss instinctively seeks restitution for the loss, and as owner of the debt has the right and obligation to seek repayment. Some losses can be recouped or replaced, such as a material item like a car or computer. Other losses cannot be recouped, such as a life or a unique item. The person who experiences loss may be tempted to fill the void with something else, anything else.

For instance, a man who lost a promotion at work attempts to fill the void with food. In another instance, a woman who lost the love of a husband tries to fill the void by making purchases. In either case, the compensatory action or item does not repay the debt or make up for the loss.

The loss cannot be recouped, but it can be resolved. The one who holds the debt can choose to release it. Once a debt is released, or forgiven, it is no longer subject to debt service. It does not accrue interest and it does not require collection.

Like other unpleasant emotions, sadness has an important role to play in the maturing process. Children experience a small loss that causes distress from which they learn to return to joy. If a mother or father cannot allow the minor distresses, children may never learn how to deal with sadness on their own.

My soul melts away for sorrow; strengthen me according to Your word! - Psalm 119:28

Chronic sadness occurs in people who are unable to resolve loss and return to joy. They accumulate losses as one sad thing triggers another and gets added to the ever-growing account. They rehearse disappointments which leads to sorrow and grief, and these stronger emotions influence their personality.

Grieve Losses

Grieving is a process through which a person resolves a loss. A great deal of study has been done on losses, such as the death of a loved one, but the principles of grieving are applicable to any loss or disappointment. Grieving is a process through which a person is restored to peace and is able to return to joy.

Because it takes life-energy to process a loss, the physical symptoms of grief can mirror other health issues. For instance, crying, headaches, lethargy, insomnia, fatigue, aches, pain, and loss of appetite are some expressions of the pain of disappointment. Abnormal behavior and unreliable decisions may arise as a person seeks comfort in other ways.

Many emotional expressions accompany grief, such as anger, worry, frustration, guilt, hopelessness, stress, and anxiety. These feelings express the grief but do not define the true identity of the grieving person. They are temporary feelings and responses to the pain.

The grieving person experiences symptoms in the spiritual realm as well. They may question their purpose in life or question the nature and character of God. They may isolate from family and community and detach from other relationships as well.

Satan tempts people with the "better off dead" lie when they are in this vulnerable condition. The lie can take several possible forms: "I would be better off dead," "You would be better off if I were dead," or "I would be better off if you were dead." Of course, the redemptive power of Jesus Christ refutes this lie, but it can feel very true in the time of pain.

Grieving is a process with an end goal in mind: to resolve the loss and be renewed in heart and mind. It is not an identity, nor a life sentence to pain, but a way to acknowledge the loss, honor the past, and accept a new beginning. The physical, emotional and spiritual symptoms of grieving resolve as the process is completed.

The grieving process is not linear or two-dimensional. It consists of phases and cycles that one goes through for each facet of loss. In a deep loss, such as the death of a loved one, there will be a primary cycle through which one comes to grip with the new reality. We call that the heavy lifting. There is also ancillary losses and disappointments to be grieved. For instance, while recognizing the death of a spouse one must also grieve the loss of future dreams and goals.

Prayer Strategy

The prayer strategy for sadness begins with identifying and acknowledging the loss, forgiving all who contributed to that loss, and asking God to fill the empty space.

    1) Acknowledge the loss.
    2) Consider what it has cost you.
    3) Receive and extend forgiveness to all who contributed to the loss.
    4) Honor the past.
    5) Ask for a renewed identity in Christ.
    6) Give thanks for a new beginning.

Take an account of what is lost or causes disappointment. In the physical realm this includes things, people, positions, and other material goods. In the emotional realm it includes rights, feelings, opportunities, expectations, and other unseen things. In the spiritual realm you may find relationships, purpose, identity, faith, hope, and love. Be as complete as possible for each phase of the grieving process and repeat as necessary.

Ask God to help you consider what the loss has cost you. Until you acknowledge the cost you cannot honor the past. It is best to complete the spiritual transactions of forgiveness while still contemplating the cost. This fulfills the first step of forgiving which is to take an account of the offenses. Receive forgiveness for your role in any part of the loss by confessing it to God and allowing Him to take the responsibility from you. Extend forgiveness to any others that contributed to the loss by confessing to God your willingness to release them from obligation and responsibility.

We honor the past by recognizing the value we enjoyed before the loss was incurred. For instance, a typical memorial service will include testimonies of good times and important contributions. Recalling the good leads to transactions of giving thanks, which are also best accomplished in confession to God.

Maturity requires change and returning to joy from the pain of loss is an important part of that change. The person you were before the loss is changed by the loss. The person you become is affected by what was lost and the new opportunities the loss has initiated. Ask God: "Who am I now?"

Expect Him to answer your question by affirming your true identity and giving insight into new ways to respond with the spiritual gifts and character traits He has placed in you.

Hopelessness

Hopelessness is an unpleasant emotion that expresses a sense of discouragement, despair, desperation and depression. This feeling comes from believing you are out of options and expecting that good cannot happen. Hopelessness is an important part of dealing with transition and grief and it sets up your return to joy. An old adage states that you do not appreciate what you have until it is gone. Hopelessness anticipates loss, recognizes what is gone, and quickens your sense of appreciation for what has not been lost.

However, chronic hopelessness leads to depression which is a form of death to the soul. The symptoms of hopelessness and depression can be characterized as death of your mind, will and emotions. Your mind may become filled with dark thoughts and befuddlement leading to a shut-down of intentional or organized thoughts. Your will to make choices and follow your purpose slows or ceases to function. Hopelessness consumes other emotions rather than allowing them to be expressed.

A feeling of hopelessness is caused by what you believe to be true. You may have experienced a difficult time or painful experience that caused you to believe that your challenges are insurmountable or that there are no solutions to the problems you are facing. You may have come to the conclusion that your life is worthless or that you are a burden to others.

Individuals who believe their death is imminent may lose hope for survival, and depression is a way for them to shut down vital functions of the emotional realm. A similar condition can arise from physical or emotional captivity where one's future is controlled by another, especially by an unloving force. The captive may feel helpless and vulnerable to the will of others. This loss of self-determination leads to a victim mentality and codependency, and a belief that they have no identity outside of someone else's influence. The belief leads to a death of their personality.

Everyone is created with a free will and the choices they make in life demonstrate their character and influence their future. Individuals of every age need to believe that they can write the story of their life by freely exercising their will. When their freedom is thwarted it can lead to disappointment, despair, and hopelessness, and they may feel oppressed, crushed, stifled, or marginalized. They may experience themselves as deficient or incapable, believing that their condition is permanent and that they will never be able to express their true identity.

Another leading cause for hopelessness is alienation. We are created to live in community, to relate with others, and to share life together. When this condition is removed it kills part of our life-purpose. Alienated individuals believe they are somehow different, either that they are unworthy or they have been cut off by some form of authority. Sadly, alienated people tend to close themselves off for fear of further pain and rejection, and their alienation is increased.

Learn from Me

Everyone can experience times of sadness and hopelessness, but the dream of a future and a hope must not die.

Prayer Strategy

> *For I know the plans I have for you, declares the LORD, plans for welfare and not for evil, to give you a future and a hope. - Jeremiah 29:11*

This promise of hope given in Jeremiah is the solution to hopelessness, but the truth must be accepted into the despairing person's heart. He or she may have memorized this verse, or others like it, but not been able to apply the truth on a personal level.

1) Ask the Lord what has triggered hopelessness.
2) Take an account of what has been lost.
3) Forgive and receive forgiveness for the loss.
4) Ask what the person believes to be true.
5) Confess the belief and ask for God's truth.
6) Ask the Lord to plant the seed of a future and a hope.

People with hopelessness or depression have trouble taking the initiative to receive prayer. The intercessor may need to lend a seed of faith or a measure of hope just to overcome the depth of despair.

When the trigger for hopelessness was a traumatic event, such as a loss or accident, the prayer strategy will follow along the lines of grieving. However, when the trigger points to a lifestyle condition, such as oppression or self-loathing, the strategy includes self-discovery and a new understanding of true identity.

Depression is a common malady which is primarily treated from a physical point of view in our culture. Medication is used to temper or relieve some of the emotional symptoms. Diet and exercise also have an effect on physical responses. Anything that alleviates the symptoms of hopelessness or sadness is good, as long as it leads to healing at the root level. Sadly, some people experience enough symptom relief that they can endure life, but they do not use this relief to their advantage to receive complete healing.

-- *Learn from Me* --

Anne could hardly pull herself together. She felt hopeless and cried all the time. Her doctor gave her a prescription but she weaned herself off of the medication because she hated the side effects. She had thoughts of self-harm and believed she, and others, would be better off if she were dead.

We prayed for a starting point, and God revealed the trigger for Anne's hopelessness. She and her husband of thirty years had separated six months before, and the relationship was doomed. She had feelings of failure, loneliness, and shame that fueled her depression. She wondered if she could go on.

We asked God to identify the specific loss at the root of this deep sadness. Anne assumed it would be the marriage, but God brought her back to her family of origin. She was the fifth of six kids, and her dad struggled with anger and depression.

Anne had a memory of a time when her dad disciplined two of her older siblings, beating them with a belt. She was young, probably five or six years old at the time, when she heard them screaming and crying downstairs. She felt guilty that they were getting beaten, and assumed she deserved it too. She was terrified that he would come up for her next. This scene typified her childhood.

"Lord, would you show Anne what she needs to know in this memory?" I prayed.

"I see Jesus in the corner of my bedroom," she stated. "I always thought I was alone. I thought I was a mistake. But Jesus is here in my bedroom."

"What is happening now?" I asked after a few moments.

"Jesus wants to hug me. I'm letting Him hug me. I'm afraid to let go. I'm afraid that He will leave me."

"Listen to what He says," I prompted.

Anne's body visibly relaxed. She responded in a calm voice, sharing that Jesus said He had always been with her and that He will stay with her.

The truth of Jesus being with her was powerful for Anne. It gave her hope. At the end of the prayer time she was still separated from her husband but she had hope because Jesus had promised to stay with her. All of the pain in the past could be forgiven and the peace of Jesus will take its place.

— Learn from Me —

Sarah had been married for four years and was desperate to get out. Her husband was domineering and she felt like she was fighting for her life. Although he had not physically abused her, she felt trapped and smothered. He would not give her any freedom to be herself, and he was never satisfied with who she was when she tried to please him. She thought she was losing her mind and she just needed to escape.

She came for prayer at the request of a friend who explained that she needed to be healed whether the marriage could be salvaged or not. She agreed she needed help though she did not put much confidence in it. She felt hopeless and desperate.

We asked God for a starting point and she confessed low self-esteem as the root problem. She had been sexually molested at a young age, abused as a young teenager, and then acted out in sexual sin during her early adult life. She had always seen herself as Gomer, Rahab, and the Samaritan woman at the well. She believed she was forever marked by her sexual sin and that she deserved whatever came to her.

I invited her to ask God for forgiveness, which she readily accepted. Then we walked through the process of forgiving those that had destroyed her innocence and abused her true identity. That was harder, but worth the effort. When she had released the offenses, it was as if a huge weight had been lifted from her shoulders.

I asked her how she felt now that she was forgiven. Her response was filled with hope where there had not been any before. She could imagine a different life. She could hope for the blessings of God. She could receive His gifts even though she did not deserve them.

That prayer time set up a new expectation for Sarah. Over the next several months God sent many messengers to give her comfort, insight, and other ideas of how to walk in this new life. Her marriage was reborn, and she looked forward to all that God might do.

— Learn from Me —

Joan attended one of my workshops on listening prayer and asked for an appointment. As we began our prayer time together she confessed feeling spiritually dead and unable to hear from God. She knew that she lived from her soul rather than her spirit, and she defaulted to her mind rather than listening to the Holy Spirit. No matter how much she tried, she could not get past this paradigm. She felt hopeless but wanted to be alive instead.

I asked God to show her what was causing this spiritual disconnect and getting in the way of her hearing Him. She did not hear any words, but immediately realized a root of fear. We explored this a little deeper, and she described it as a fear of the opinions of others. She had always strived to do the right thing for sake of appearance and believed that her acceptance was dependent on her performance. Her Catholic upbringing and strict legalism in her family of origin had set up this mindset.

She suffered from hopelessness because she could never measure up to the standards placed on her by others. In part, she felt like a constant failure because her husband was an alcoholic and in poor health. She had exhausted herself trying to help him get better, but he continued to decline. "What do people think of me for not being able to take better care of him?" she wondered.

I invited her to ask God for forgiveness for accepting the responsibility for her husband's condition though she did not have the authority to control it. This spiritual transaction brought her great relief. Then I invited her to ask for forgiveness for being guided by fear instead of love, to which she quickly agreed and expressed a new freedom in her heart as a result.

"Joan, are you willing to let God give you instruction for your life now that you have been forgiven for following the opinions of others?" I asked.

"Yes! And I want to follow Him with my spirit instead of my mind," she confessed.

Her heart shifted as she repeated those words in a prayer of confession. Suddenly she had a ray of hope inside. She knew that God was in control and had a plan for her and her husband. She was willing to let Him lead.

"Thank you for praying with me. Now I know God has a way for me to live, and I know I can listen to Him," she said as we finished our time together.

Only God can restore hope to the hopeless.

Depression

Depression is a common mood disorder that affects how a person feels, thinks, and makes decisions. The symptoms of depression are despondency, dejection, and chronic sadness or hopelessness. The symptoms must be present for at least two weeks for a diagnosis of depression. If the condition persists for more than two years it is considered major or clinical depression.

The cause of depression may be physical. Hormones play an important role in managing moods, and an imbalance can lead to symptoms of depression. For example, proper production of estrogen and progesterone can be interrupted by menopause or postpartum recovery. Thyroid problems, diabetes, and chronic pain are also linked to depression. Drugs can be prescribed as depressants to lower neurotransmission levels, and other drugs can cause depression as a side effect. Substance abuse can also trigger these symptoms.

Pray for physical healing. Ask God to reveal the root cause of the problem and then follow His leading. If it is a chemical imbalance within the body, ask Him to set it right and return it to proper function. If the origin is from another disease or condition, pray for healing in that area and expect the symptoms of depression to clear up as the healing takes effect.

Diet and exercise have a significant impact on depression, for good or bad. We can follow God's rules for healthy living and come into compliance with His precepts. Proper nutrition fuels the body and helps it work according to its design, and the right balance of exercise and rest keeps us going strong. Be prepared to lead the person in a prayer of forgiveness to break sinful patterns or habits.

The cause of depression is more often emotional. Past physical, sexual, or emotional abuse can increase vulnerability to major depression. Personal conflicts, relational distress, and disputes can also lead to depression. Death or a loss triggers grief, and incomplete grieving can result in clinical depression. Many personal problems invoke the symptoms associated with depression.

The trauma of abandonment, rejection, or betrayal leads to conflict which causes pain. The soul, comprised of the mind, will, and emotions, tries to resolve the conflict which can lead to mental and emotional fatigue. If the person does not get positive results they may give up or withdraw. Sadness then becomes hopelessness which in turn becomes depression.

The prayer strategy begins by asking God to reveal the root or cause of this sadness. He may bring a specific traumatic memory to their mind or He may use a representative one. He is always gentle and knows exactly how to bring about complete healing. We have seen Him begin by resolving a relatively minor conflict which then led the person to apply His truth to many more severe conflicts. We have also seen Him tackle the big trauma first and everything else falls in line.

Depression can be the result of physical, emotional, or spiritual abuse. The only way to resolve the debt is for the one who suffered to forgive the abuser. Depression can also be due to constant conflict or interpersonal relationships, which can be resolved by forgiving the offenders. In either case, the emotional distress is healed with mind renewal and reconciliation with God. The offenders may not have a role to play in the healing, nor is it dependent on them. God heals the hurt by supernaturally resolving the conflict.

Finally, depression is a normal part of the grieving process. As mentioned above, clinical depression is defined by symptoms that persist for two years or more. Sometimes the solution to clinical depression is the completion of the grieving process.

> *To comfort all who mourn, to grant to those who mourn in Zion— to give them a beautiful headdress instead of ashes, the oil of gladness instead of mourning, the garment of praise instead of a faint spirit; that they may be called oaks of righteousness, the planting of the LORD, that He may be glorified. · Isaiah 61:2-3*

Sadness, hopelessness, and depression belong to those who mourn, but the LORD has a new future in mind for them. He will restore.

Chapter Fifteen:
The Mind of Christ

"For who has understood the mind of the Lord so as to instruct Him?" But we have the mind of Christ. - 1 Corinthians 2:16

Why do some prayers work, and others do not?

Why do some good and faithful Christians experience chronic pain, even though they have been forgiven and trust Jesus as their Savior and Healer?

How do you know what to pray when you intercede for others?

We have been privileged to pray with many people through our ministry, and we have learned wonderful things about the way God answers prayer. However, not everyone we pray with receives healing. The questions above are ones we have asked and discussed with others.

The Will of God

And this is the confidence that we have toward Him, that if we ask anything according to His will He hears us. And if we know that He hears us in whatever we ask, we know that we have the requests that we have asked of Him. - *1 John 5:14-15*

The Bible is full of promises to claim, and this verse provides a primary one for prayer ministry. "We have whatever we ask according to His will." There should be no confusion about this promise: when we ask God for something He wants to give us, we can be assured that He will give it to us. Along the same lines, if we ask God to do something that He wants to do, we can be certain that He will do it.

Tom asked during a prayer appointment, "How do I know if I'm praying according to God's will or mine?" I had just shared this promise with him because he wanted to pray with great faith.

"The only time you have to distinguish between your will and God's is when the two differ," I replied. "As long as your will and God's are the same, it doesn't matter. When a variation exists, go with God's. His is always better."

It takes effort to know God's will, but it begins in your relationship with Him, not with the content or structure of the prayer. If you do not know His will, it means you do not know Him in that particular area. You learn His will by studying His character and nature. He is always true and perfect and you can count on Him to remain in character.

The key for powerful prayer is to get my will to agree with His. For example, I may pray for relief from physical symptoms because they are painful, but it would be better for me to pray for truth. The truth sets me free, according to John 8:36, because it reconciles me with God's character at the root level. Symptom relief may only mask a problem, but healing brings me back into agreement with God's ways.

We gain the mind of Christ through a process of mind renewal.

> *Do not be conformed to this world, but be transformed by the renewal of your mind, that by testing you may discern what is the will of God, what is good and acceptable and perfect. - Romans 12:2*

Mind renewal changes our way of thinking, adjusts our frame of reference, until we know and agree with the will of God. The world's way of perceiving is surrendered and God's perspective takes its place.

We are reconciled to Him and made new.

> *Therefore, if anyone is in Christ, he is a new creation. The old has passed away; behold, the new has come. All this is from God, who through Christ reconciled us to Himself and gave us the ministry of reconciliation. - 2 Corinthians 5:17-18*

In our newness we can proclaim that we have the mind of Christ. We share His thoughts, feelings, desires, and purposes. Whatever we ask the Father we know we can expect to receive because it is the same thing Jesus would ask if He were on earth again.

Whatever you ask in My name, this I will do, that the Father may be glorified in the Son. If you ask Me anything in My name, I will do it. - John 14:13-14

Healing prayer is listening prayer because it is led by the Holy Spirit.

And He who searches hearts knows what is the mind of the Spirit, because the Spirit intercedes for the saints according to the will of God. - Romans 8:27

As we pray, we must listen to the Spirit inside for guidance. He can speak to our spirit when we have opened the channel of communication. We must also listen to the words that come out of our mouth as we pray. The Holy Spirit can speak through us things we did not know or decide to pray on our own. By eavesdropping on God, listening in our spirit, we can discern what is His will, what is good and acceptable and perfect.

For who knows a person's thoughts except the spirit of that person, which is in him? So also no one comprehends the thoughts of God except the Spirit of God. - 1 Corinthians 2:11

At times, when you pray with someone, the Holy Spirit reveals things in prayer that you would have no other way of knowing. God uses this tool to build confidence in His word. If I speak to a person, the message is filtered by their mind and interpreted by their paradigm. On the other hand, God speaks to their heart and then they know His word is true.

— Learn from Me —

We sometimes use a "prayer chair" in our small groups so anyone can receive intercessory prayer from the others. The one who sits in the chair might share a need or concern and then a few others gather around to pray, often with the laying on of hands.

One evening a young lady sat in the chair but was unable to share her need. Each time she tried to speak out, her voice would fail her. The others in the group began to pray as the Spirit led. As I recall, three or four people prayed and there was a new calmness in the young woman.

A short pause ensued, and then a new member of the group began to read a Psalm. He personalized the verses with her name and softly gave a message of mercy, forgiveness, and restoration. He had no way of knowing that she was racked with guilt and seeking confirmation from God that her sins were forgiven. Not only did God speak those words to her, but He did so in a way that she knew came directly from Him. If someone who knew her story had shared those same words it would not have had as powerful an effect.

"You have no idea," she said as she rose from her seat.

"You're right," he answered. "I have no idea."

Intercessory prayer is led by the Spirit, and we must learn to discern when the thoughts are our thoughts, His thoughts, or the same thoughts.

Strength of Soul

When we are not being led by the Spirit we are being led by our soul, which is made up of our mind, will and emotions. Being led by your soul means you act according to what you think, what you want, and how you feel. The way of the world is soul-led rather than spirit-led, and strength of soul is determined by how much you depend on it.

The soul is resilient, and in normal day to day activities you may be led by any one of its parts. In some circumstances you trust your mind, reason, and rationale. In other situations, you might rely on your senses or gut feelings. Alternatively, you might be guided by your choices or responsibilities.

However, everyone has a default setting. When things get rough, when push comes to shove, you rely on one aspect of your soul over the others. Think about what that "go to" setting is for you. To have the mind of Christ requires that you surrender your soul and respond through your spirit. When you know the symptoms of your soulish behavior you will find the act of surrender easier to accomplish.

Mind

The mind is the seat of knowledge which relies on information, logic, and conclusions. The mind is quick to judge, obsessed with right and wrong, and can be fed by the Tree of Knowledge of Good and Evil. It defies faith and demands answers that can be tested and evaluated. As such it is susceptible to corruption of a faulty worldview.

The symptoms of mind-led soulish behavior are a reliance on information, black and white judgment, and strong opinions. These opinions become guiding principles and are vetted through argument or logic. We may have this as our default setting if we tend to refer to authoritative sources for facts, use our logic or reason to form opinions, and are dogmatic in our viewpoint.

The mind that is led by the Spirit has been renewed and reconciled to a perfect worldview.

Will

The will is defined by what we want and what we choose. Willful people are committed to their commitments, sensitive to responsibility, and subject to their whims. We demand the right to choose and expect everyone to be bound by our choices. Will is expressed by choice but defined by purpose. Our will is susceptible to evil when it conflicts with the purposes of God.

The characteristics of will-led soulish behavior are decisiveness, stubbornness, determination, and responsibility. We want what we want and are willing to pay anything to have it. We can be impulsive and willing to move forward without reason or encouragement. Our will can mimic faith, but it is grounded on our purpose rather than God's truth.

The will that is led by the Spirit has been surrendered and made obedient to God's will and purposes.

Emotions

The emotions are defined by how you feel and what you sense. They can motivate intuitively by operating from a gut feeling. They are sensitive to the impact a choice will have on self and others, and quickly assign favorable or unpleasant values to feelings. Emotions are personal and subject to what we believe to be true. A faulty paradigm can trigger unstable emotions.

The symptoms of emotion-led soulish behavior are sensitivity and expression. Some decisions are made to avoid unpleasant emotions and others to pursue pleasant ones. Since emotions can change rapidly, the guidance of the emotion-led soul can be unpredictable.

The emotions that are led by the Spirit are ones that agree with the Lord. A godly and true emotion is any that would be the same as the response Jesus would have in similar circumstances. If our heart is broken by the consequences of sin in the world, we are sharing the same emotion Jesus described as He looked over Jerusalem. If our heart is happy by the return of a sinner, we are experiencing what Jesus, and a thousand angels, are also feeling.

Walk by the Spirit

But I say, walk by the Spirit, and you will not gratify the desires of the flesh. - Galatians 5:16

I have a mental picture of a couple walking, hand in hand, on a nice afternoon. We do not know where they are going, but they are obviously in agreement. The pace is comfortable and they enjoy one another's company. It is a metaphor for walking by the Spirit.

When we have the mind of Christ, our every thought, feeling and impulse is the same as His. We are headed in the same direction, according to the same purpose. We can slip our hand in His for comfort or pleasure, and we enjoy the journey as we share our experiences of it. In this picture there is room for individuality as well as commonality.

This union is one that we maintain. He has reconciled us to Himself, and we are a new creation. All the sin and shame of the past has been forgiven and nothing can separate us from His love. We are in a sweet spot to be enjoyed.

Reconsider the illustration of Slim and Coin, yoked together to do the work, and enjoying one another's companionship. The yoke represents our shared purpose and our proximity represents our relationship. When we are connected like this we work and act as one. We have the mind of Christ.

Give Way

I visited some Christian friends in Trinidad several years ago, and while touring the countryside I saw a traffic sign. I knew by the shape that it was a yield sign, but the words printed on it were "give way." I was struck by the simplicity of that synonym, and it helped me understand the action of yielding.

When you are in opposition to the purposes or will of God, give way. Do not strain ahead or hang back in the yoke, instead surrender your will and accept His. When you have made a commitment that goes against His instructions, give way. Do not pull against the yoke but make a new choice and do things the way He suggests. When you take something personally and have an emotional response that is not the same as what God feels in that moment, give way. Release your emotions and wonder why He feels differently.

We walk by the Spirit by being sensitive to this unity. Whenever disagreement arises, however slight, choose to give way and you will always be in step with Him.

When He Checks

At times our mind, will or emotions will disconnect us from the Spirit. This misalignment can happen when we think about the wrong things, act in self-interest, or pursue wrong emotions. If we pay attention, we will recognize that He has put a check in our spirit. It may be as subtle as a twinge or passing question mark.

When He checks, stop immediately. If you ignore the quiet hint you will find yourself pulling away from His side. The longer it takes for you to recognize the change, the further you will have strayed. He is willing to call you back but sticking close to Him is the sweet spot.

Spiritual Disciplines

We can do some things to encourage our walk with God by engaging in practices that help us maintain our relationship with Him. If we do them out of religious obligation we get no benefit, but if we do them with a sincere heart it makes a difference in our life.

Quiet Time

Set aside a little time each day to spend with the Lord. Use this quiet time to meditate, pray and listen, read His word, and ponder His thoughts. Schedule this time in a way that it is hard to interrupt. Many people prefer to do this first thing in the morning before other cares and concerns take up space in the day. Others like to do this at the end of the day as things quiet down and they prepare to sleep.

Meet with the Lord. A relationship grows well when we meet and share ideas, hopes, dreams, and all other aspects of life.

Sabbath Rest

Set aside a little time each week to spend with the Lord. A sabbath rest is one day per week spent without the cares and toils of the world. It is a time for rest and restoration. Without this break it is very hard to maintain a healthy perspective. When you take this break, it is a natural way to obey Jesus and "cast your cares on Him."

Evidence exists that our physical and emotional health are affected by this spiritual discipline as well. The body needs a chance to repair and recover, and one day per week is the Manufacturer's recommendation. Our emotions need a break too, and by taking this time of intentional rest we find ourselves being reset to joy and peace.

Personal Renewal Days

Once every six weeks it is good to take a day off to reassess your life and walk. I begin by refreshing my purpose statement to make sure it is still in line with God's will. Then I review my goals to make sure they are consistent with my purpose. Finally, I review my calendar to confirm that it accommodates my goals.

Use your personal renewal days as a tool to provide direction. I have discovered areas of my life that had pulled away from God while doing this review. It is much easier to change an error while it is still young, rather than after it has hardened into a lifestyle.

Healing Communities

And let us consider how to stir up one another to love and good works, not neglecting to meet together, as is the habit of some, but encouraging one another, and all the more as you see the Day drawing near. - Hebrews 10:24-25

Healing happens in community. It is up to you to develop a community where you can be stirred up to love, good works and encouragement. You may be able to join an existing community, such as a church or small group, or you may need to create your own. Remember that the body of Christ is displayed in groups, and the gifts of the Spirit are sprinkled around so each can strengthen others.

Church of the Heart

Our friend, Dan Mayhew, asks this question: "With whom has your Father called you to be the church? Remember, your 'church of the heart' is not a place you go, but a people you cherish. The new commandment of Jesus is to love one another in ways that others can notice."

A church of the heart may be a small group of like-minded Christ-followers that gets together for worship, fellowship, and encouragement. It may look like a local church with a building and organizational structure. It might also look like a band of

243

brothers meeting in a restaurant. It might look like a Bible study that meets in a living room once a week. It might look like a far-flung group of dedicated believers that meet by phone or computer.

The key ingredient of a church of the heart is acknowledgement that Christ is the head, and the members are the body. As each member walks in the Spirit, the body will move according to the will of Christ.

Trusted Advisors

Align yourself with peers who can help you hear from the Lord and be accountable. In an abundance of counselors there is safety (Proverbs 11:14), and we need good friends to help us pay attention to the Spirit.

Also cultivate relationships with elders from whom you can receive godly advice. These trusted advisors are recognized by their wisdom more than their age. They do not spout off an opinion but can be trusted to inquire of the Lord and share what they hear.

Special Resources

And He gave the apostles, the prophets, the evangelists, the shepherds and teachers, to equip the saints for the work of ministry, for building up the body of Christ. - *Ephesians 4:11-12*

The Apostle Paul referred to apostles, prophets, evangelists, pastors, and teachers as roles needed to equip the saints and build up the body of Christ. Look around your community of believers and identify the ones that fill each of these roles. If any are missing, make it your mission to discover them and establish a relationship. A person cannot effectively do the work of ministry or mature into Christ-likeness without them.

Find ways to pray together. We have begun a School of Prayer that meets once a week to put intercession into practice. We begin with a teaching component to introduce a principle or technique for effective prayer ministry. Then we break into groups of four or five and pray together. Each week people receive prayer and are healed. Each week people practice praying for others and build confidence in their ability to hear God and act as witness to His miracles. Each week people are introduced to healing prayer. I recommend joining or initiating such a group in your location.

Find ways to serve together. We have a semi-annual meeting for Kingdom Ministries. People from various ministries gather for corporate prayer and mutual encouragement. As we meet, share, and pray together we get a glimpse at what God is up to on a global level. I recommend making an alliance with other ministries so you can be encouraged together.

Find ways to seek the Lord together. We use the term "Prayer Summit" to describe a time of corporate prayer. This is an opportunity for a group of people to meet and practice listening prayer together. These meetings last anywhere from three hours to three days and are guided entirely by the Holy Spirit. No agenda is established in advance but the Spirit provides direction.

One of the benefits of corporate prayer is that God reveals His truth in community, just as He heals in community. Sometimes He gives part of a picture to one person and the rest to another. Unless you are listening and sharing together you do not get the whole message. At other times He uses one person to confirm a message heard by another. This builds confidence and establishes truth.

Storm the Gates

And I tell you, you are Peter, and on this rock I will build my church, and the gates of hell shall not prevail against it. - Matthew 16:18

We do not wage war as the world does. The medical community focuses on the physical realm and is often satisfied with symptom management. Their strategy is limited to what the caregivers are able to measure and prove with tests, and the battle is waged in the physical realm. However, you cannot sedate an evil spirit, it must be removed by spiritual authority.

We do not wage war as the world does. The mental health community focuses on the emotional realm and is often satisfied with making a pain or conflict manageable. Their strategy is limited by the prevailing worldview of the culture. However, you cannot reprogram a law or tolerate an argument, it must be taken captive and made obedient to Christ.

We demolish strongholds with spiritual warfare, and then we replace their rules with God as the Highest authority. We destroy arguments by taking them captive and force them to surrender to the Truth. We tear down every pretension by identifying the false belief and replacing it with truth through mind renewal.

We are the church, the body of Christ. When we wage war in the heavenly places with divine power, the gates of hell cannot stand against us!

> ... But the people who know their God shall stand firm and take action. - Daniel 11:32

We have the mind of Christ. We have the Holy Spirit within us forever. We are united with God through Jesus, and He gives us instruction of what we are to do and what we are to say. We are prayer warriors, and we are able to stand firm and take action.

We pray that God will bless you with this blessing:

> Now to Him who is able to do far more abundantly than all that we ask or think, according to the power at work within us, to Him be glory in the church and in Christ Jesus throughout all generations, forever and ever. Amen. - Ephesians 3:20-21

Index

Resources

About the Authors

Calvin and Julie Tadema were called into full time ministry in 2004 and started offering healing prayer through Master's Mind Ministry in 2007. The ministry was built on individual prayer appointments for healing in the spiritual, emotional and physical realms. They also teach about listening prayer, reconciliation, and gaining a deeper relationship with God. They conduct workshops, seminars and retreats to share the good news about God's mercy and to equip others in healing prayer. More information and many resources are freely available on the website: www.mastersmindministry.org.

Other Titles

These books are also available through Two Worlds Press (www.twoworldsmedia.com):

Heal Me, O Lord: The Christian's handbook to personal wholeness through healing prayer

By Calvin Tadema - 2015.

The simple prayer of faith found in Jeremiah 17:14 is your invitation to confident healing prayer. The God that gives salvation to all who ask is the LORD who promises to heal. This instructional handbook is a clear guide for effective and powerful prayer that leads to reconciliation, healing, and peace. It is filled with examples and testimonies of God's supernatural ways to encourage and strengthen your prayer life and your relationship with Him.

The Ancient Deceptions: Uncover the oldest tricks in The Book

By Jody Mayhew and Julie Tadema - 2014.

Lies ... When we believe them, they may as well be true. When we discover the truth, deception loses its power.

Learn from Me

The Ancient Deceptions helps you uncover the lies that have been around since the first humans believed them and shows you how to keep from falling for the oldest tricks in The Book.

Marriage Rx: Prescription for a radical marriage

By Dan & Jody Mayhew, Calvin & Julie Tadema - 2013.

Marriage Rx is a code name that came as a response to the news that yet another Christian marriage was headed for divorce. We agreed that the schemes of the enemy included the destruction of marriages, derailing those that have been called to serve, and taking out those that should be spiritual leaders. What was God's prescription for this epidemic?

We went away to a quiet place to pray and seek His face. Out of that prayer time came a picture of God's intentions for marriage. This book is not a new list of actions and behaviors to help husbands and wives get along better, it is a description of the character and identity of God reflected through married Christians living as examples of His nature. *Marriage Rx* is about your marriage - all of our marriages - but more than that, it is about His marriage: Christ and His church.

Speaking and Teaching

Calvin and Julie Tadema regularly teach workshops, classes, seminars and retreats in the Pacific Northwest and by invitation to churches and groups around the country and internationally.

Go to www.mastersmindministry.org for free information and support materials, such as articles, newsletters, worksheets, audio and video presentations, and upcoming training classes. Use this site to inquire about their availability to speak or teach in your community.

Master's Mind Ministry
21811 NE 164th St
Brush Prairie, WA 98606

Endnotes

[1] One of our favorite treatments of this topic comes from the excellent book: *Wealth, Riches and Money*, by Craig Hill and Earl Pitts, Littleton, CO, 2001.

[2] We wrote extensively about kinds of relating in our prior book on marriage, co-authored with the Mayhews: *Marriage Rx: Prescription for a radical marriage*, Two Worlds Press, 2013, Chapter 5.

[3] Townsend, John, *Hiding from Love: How to change the withdrawal patterns that isolate and imprison you*, Zondervan, Grand Rapids, MI, 1991, 1996.

[4] Ziemann, Adam E. et al, *The Amygdala Is a Chemosensor that Detects Carbon Dioxide and Acidosis to Elicit Fear Behavior*, Cell, Volume 139, Issue 5, 1012 - 1021, Nov. 25, 2009.

[5] Klein DF, *False suffocation alarms, spontaneous panics, and related conditions. An integrative hypothesis*, Arch. Gen. Psychiatry, 1993 Apr; 50(4):306-17.

97164324R10139

Made in the USA
Columbia, SC
11 June 2018